HOT PAPER

Also by Gerald Astor

The New York Cops
The Charge Is Rape
". . . And a Credit to His Race"

HOT PAPER

Gerald Astor

SATURDAY REVIEW PRESS | E. P. DUTTON & CO., INC.
New York

The names of some of the persons in this book have been changed. The incidents are, however, completely factual and all participants are real.

LIBRARY OF CONGRESS CATALOGING IN PUBLICATION DATA

Astor, Gerald, 1926–
Hot Paper

I. Title.
PZ4.A84157Gr [PS3551.S69]   813'.5'4   75-16155

Published simultaneously in Canada by Clarke, Irwin & Company Limited, Toronto and Vancouver
ISBN: 0-8415-0405-9

To
my father who taught me the meaning of honesty

Contents

HOT PAPER

I

The World Series Caper

On Thursday, October 16, 1969, at 3:17 P.M. New York Mets leftfielder Cleon Jones secured a fly ball hit by Dave Johnson of the Baltimore Orioles. After only eight years of life, destiny's brats had won their first World Series.

It was, otherwise, a routine day. Three Americans, Dr. Alfred D. Hershey, Dr. Salvador E. Luria, and Dr. Max Delbrück, shared the Nobel prize for medicine. The front page of *The New York Times* carried a story on Craig Badiali and Joan Fox, a pair of Blackwood, New Jersey, 17-year-olds who hooked a vacuum cleaner hose to the exhaust of an automobile and died of carbon monoxide suffocation in protest against the continuing war in Vietnam. On October 15, tens of thousands of people had gathered in Washington, D.C., for Moratorium Day. In Paris, the North Vietnamese suggested that the United States and the indigenous Vietnamese opposition to Saigon negotiate a settlement without representatives of either North or South Vietnam. The notion was unacceptable to the U.S.

From the U.S. military command came the good news that only eighty-two Americans had been killed in the previous week, one of the lowest levels of the last three years. The statistics on Vietnamese dead did not make *The New York Times.* And in Washington, President Richard Nixon spoke of his plans to resist inflation.

But on October 16, for New York City, the victory of the Mets blotted out Vietnam, the nine-month-old Nixon administration, and even the normal run of business for Thursday afternoon. Many teachers, unable to attract attention over the hum of transistor radios tuned to the broadcast from Shea Stadium, had suspended classes. In saloons and restaurants, patrons lingered over the TV, the proprietors sold few drinks as the early afternoon baseball drama, like some intimate nightclub act, demanded too much empathy to permit the clinking of glasses, the shouted orders. And not all of the bar residents were the ordinary customers. "I'd never been in a bar before but I just had to see it on TV," said a 14-year-old boy who entered one place and was allowed to remain until the alcohol began to flow at the end of the game.

In company conference rooms, in executive suites and lounges, employees and management broke away from their tasks to catch the contest. Some of the TV spectators abandoned all pretense of work; others observed intermittently, carrying back the latest information to their colleagues who'd remained at desks, machines, and counters.

On the seventeenth floor of 23 Wall Street, the home of the Morgan Guaranty Trust Company, in the large bullpen area known as the "custody section" of the bank, something like four hundred people worked or moved frequently through the area, combining business with viewing the game on a television set in a lounge on the twelfth floor. A loud-speaker system carried the inning-by-inning results to those unable to tear themselves away from their desks. The Person, like the other hands at

Morgan Guaranty, followed the exploits of the local darlings but the game fed different considerations into The Person's mind.

The World Series had not depressed trading in Wall Street for the day; it was a 19,500,000-share day while the previous days saw 15,000,000 shares traded. The volume threatened to bury firms such as Morgan Guaranty Trust under deep paper drifts. And the international traders like the Bank of Japan or the distant domestic operators such as the Commercial Bank of Memphis or the Toledo National Trust continued to buy and sell even as the Orioles and Mets struggled. In the custody room millions upon millions of dollars worth of certificates continued to move in the established flow patterns. As The Person handled these paper instruments, some of which bore noneradicable labels of ownership while others were as negotiable as ten-dollar bills, it was obvious that a light layer of confusion or at least distraction pervaded the custody area. The behavior or actions of The Person were less likely to be noticed by fellow workers laboring with their own jobs while fascinated by the doings of the Mets.

The victory at Shea Stadium sent some of the crowd of 57,397 fans pouring onto the turf in a frantic attempt to offer tactile affection for the day's heroes. In the office buildings of New York, however, such release at 3:17 in the afternoon was not company policy. In lieu of early dismissal, many workers gathered at the windows of those buildings old-fashioned enough still to have windows that could be opened and hailed the day's exploits with traditional showers of business-machine cards, ticker tape, toilet tissue, and stationery.

Nowhere was there more paper to shed, nor perhaps a greater density of buildings with windows that opened onto the narrow streets, than in the financial district located on the easterly part of Manhattan's foot. A great blizzard of paper floated into the hollows of Wall Street; the rapid pace of stock-exchange trading means an extremely high quotient of obsolescent memoranda, including the ticker tape whose value is as ephemeral as the breath that precedes the current one. Moreover, as the exchange closed dutifully at 3 P.M. that day, a large reservoir of individuals whose services were no longer required for the business of the day were let loose and the Wall Street caverns became thick with both paper and celebrants, cavorting in an Indian summer sunshine of 60 degrees.

For those employees and executives still required to finish out the day, work took a secondary importance to the fun of playing eyewitness to what an old-timer called the biggest celebration to hit the area since news of Lindbergh's arrival in Paris forty-two years before. The alfresco hoopla surpassed the parades tended astronauts, whose grand ticker-tape routes never wound through the financial district.

The custody room at Morgan Guaranty Trust offered a fine view of the goings-on. To forestall an egregious accidental or purposeful emptying out of the vital paper instruments, the windows, except for one, do not open. Unable to add to the materials of the street galas, the workers on the seventeenth floor flitted from their desks to intermittent views of the freer souls below. On the steps of the Sub-Treasury Building, which faces one side of the Morgan Guaranty (the New York Stock Exchange is across the street on another side of the bank) where George Washington's statue holds out his hand—presumably in exposition, not supplication—the partying moved toward its peak. A crowd gathered on the paper-strewn steps while a young man pounded out a beat upon an upturned coffee urn from one of Schrafft's restaurant carts that rolled between buildings with coffee and snacks for employees. By 4:40 in the afternoon, the police, however, began to feel that the euphoria might develop into trouble unless it was dampened. A number of irate motorists had appeared at the Old Slip police station, which was responsible for the law and order of the area, to protest the behavior of ex-uberant individuals who walked across hoods and roofs of cars stalled in the throngs of people on the streets.

The paper had drifted to ankle- and even knee-deep piles and the cops began shooing people toward the sub-ways. Humans do not live in the financial district, a ves-tigial reminder of man's losing battle to separate himself from Mammon. The music-makers and the audience on the steps of the Sub-Treasury dispersed. George Washing-ton was left with a sign: GOD IS NOT DEAD. HE IS ALIVE AND PLAYING FOR THE METS.

The spectators returned from their window vantage points for a final light thrust at the day's work. Then it was quitting time. In the custody section of the MGTC, the certificates still awaiting processing were heaped on desks and in work baskets; millions of dollars worth of securities owned by Morgan itself or entrusted to its care went into the locked temporary storage trunks on the floor, for re-trieval in the morning. The room would be secured and guarded for the evening but it was simply sound banking not to leave anything valuable lying about at night.

It was time for The Person to leave, too. But the tidying up and the safeguarding of the valuables owned or en-trusted to Morgan Guaranty was only of ironic interest to The Person.

For as The Person left the premises, $13,194,000 in Treasury bills, also left the building. The largest recorded theft of negotiable securities in the history of U.S. finance had just occurred, somewhat coincidentally with the great-est upset of the year in sports.*

---

* In 1974, the Chase Manhattan Bank was hit for a $15,000,000 theft which surpassed the figure for the 1969 robbery, but at least partially because of what happened to Morgan Guaranty, the theft was discovered swiftly and no losses were suffered.

II

Considerations

Since 1929, the United States government has sold Treasury bills as a means to procure cash for government obligations. Treasury bills are noninterest-bearing notes that are payable to the bearer, like checks made out to "cash." They are sold more or less weekly on a discount basis and the income from them amounts to the difference between the purchase price at discount and full maturity value. Sold at auction, the bills are short-term notes with maturity on a thirteen-week, twenty-six week, or nine-month basis. In 1970, the lowest denominations of $1,000 and $5,000 were eliminated because the Treasury and financial institutions felt small-scale investors were too much trouble. Treasury bills currently are issued for $10,000, $100,000, $500,000, and $1,000,000.

As a highly liquid short-term investment, Treasury bills have proven a most useful tool to large financial institutions and to anyone dealing in big sums of money. Banks, brokerage houses, even foreign governments deal in Treasury bills. In 1969 there were around $90,000,000,000 in Treasury bills circulating through the financial community. One further note: because they are discount obligations, the profit is collected before the date of maturity. All trading or conversion of Treasury bills normally ends on the date of maturity. Anyone who presents a Treasury bill after the maturity date naturally engenders suspicion, for no legitimate owner ordinarily holds onto the things after they cease to earn money.

Treasury bills look much like stock certificates. A bill is slightly more than nine inches long and just under six and one-half inches wide. The Bureau of Engraving makes them up, using both the intaglio process (a printing technique) and plain typography. The paper is similar to that used for currency except that the Treasury bill paper does not contain the distinctive fibers of money.

On the face of the bill is a border design, a portrait of a former Secretary of the Treasury, the denomination of the bill, and the due and payable dates. The back of the bill bears the amount of the bill, the due and payable specification, along with an engraving of an eagle.

The $1,000 denomination had Hugh McCulloch, Secretary of the Treasury under President Abraham Lincoln, on the front with a green eagle on the back. On the $5,000 was John G. Carlisle (Grover Cleveland); the back was red. On the $10,000 is John Sherman (Rutherford B. Hayes) with a purple eagle. Lyman Gage (William McKinley) marks the $15,000 note and his eagle is brown. Carter Glass (Woodrow Wilson) fronts the $50,000 note with a pink eagle. The $100,000 bill bears Albert Gallatin (Thomas Jefferson) and a blue eagle. William Crawford (James Madison) is worth $500,000 and his eagle is green. The $1,000,000 bill carries Oliver Wolcott (George Washington) with a gray eagle.

The bills are sold at auctions about forty times a year.

Banks such as Morgan Guaranty Trust deal in T bills, buy-ing as much as $25,000,000 worth at a time, then selling them to customers or keeping them as interest-earning assets.

Because of their dollar amounts and because they can technically be cashed or traded by whoever has possession of them, Treasury bills are not casually carried around in the wallets of corporate presidents or international bankers. They travel by registered mail or bonded messenger but more often than not they travel on paper only. The Bank of Tokyo might swap U.S. dollars accrued from the sale of Toyotas for Treasury bills that will be only slightly less liquid than dollars but which will earn a return while the Bank of Tokyo determines how it wants to employ its funds. A Memphis bank like the Bank of Commerce will increase its liquidity by exchanging long-term municipals for T bills. Morgan Guaranty acts as both a dealer and a custodian in such transactions. The T bills never leave the premises at 23 Wall Street; they simply shuffle from one account to the other.

As the fifth largest financial institution in the U.S., the Morgan Guaranty Trust—how the name rolls off the tongue, dripping intimations of fiduciary impregna-bility—does a considerable business in the trading and management of Treasury bills. The hyperthyroid J. P. Morgan established his private bank, J. P. Morgan and Co., in 1861. The Guaranty Indemnity Co. of New York received its charter in 1864. It became the Guaranty Trust Co. of New York in 1896. After the turn of the century some Morgan partners bought an interest in the Guaranty Trust. The institutions operated separately but often in concert until 1959 when a merger created Morgan Guar-anty Trust Company. J. P. Morgan's offices had always been at the corner of Broad and Wall; he had the current building built on the site of his original offices in 1914.

The tall adjacent building that houses most of the employees was erected in 1928, bought by J. P. Morgan and Co. in 1955.

On October 16, 1969, the securities processing center of the Morgan Guaranty Trust was operating strictly on a "functional basis," in the words of Vice President Carl Klemme. Items handled on the seventeenth floor, whether they consisted of stocks and bonds bearing the owners' names or of paper that indicated the bearer qualified as owner, all shuffled through the same mill. (Since the theft, however, Morgan Guaranty Trust has altered its procedures, separating out the government securities from other types for special treatment.)

The security processing department then, as now, had two entry doors. In 1969, a single guard controlled the passages. Posted at one, he monitored the other door by means of a closed circuit television camera. Admittance to the room required an identification badge. There were one hundred thirty-five people at work in the unit that World Series afternoon. Among them was Ronald Duffy, a chunky man built like a high school football guard who failed to grow taller.

Ronald Duffy grew up in Brooklyn's Bedford-Stuyvesant before it turned into a black ghetto slum. "My father was an alcoholic," says Duffy. "I went to Alexander Hamilton, a vocational high school, where I studied electricity and carpentry, but the first job I could get was as a messenger for the bank. My mother said, 'That's nice, a good clean job and you'll be finished at 3 P.M.' Hah," snorts Duffy. "I worked my ass off, sometimes six days a week. I live on Staten Island and I'd take the 5 A.M. ferry to get to work in the morning and I'd take the 1 A.M. ferry to get home."

But by such efforts, Ronald Duffy had climbed the Morgan Guaranty Trust ladder to the post of assistant secretary in charge of the delivery section. "That covered commercial paper and treasuries," explains Duffy. "New issues were a big thing then. People who dealt in governments would go into new issues for a few quick bucks and then back out again, so the business in Treasury bills was brisk."

Among the organizations who were customers of the Morgan Guaranty Trust and participated in Treasury bill transactions that October day were the Bank of Tokyo, the Toledo (Ohio) Trust, and the Bank of Commerce in Memphis, Tennessee. The traffic flow called for the Treasury bills to pass through the security incoming section where they were marked for deposit in the accounts of these three customers. The established procedure at Morgan Guaranty dictated that every item be ticketed as to whether it only left the vaults in the basement of the bank or came from an outside organization. At the incoming section notation would be made of the arrival of the security, and as it went to outgoing there would be another piece of documentation. When it disappeared back into the vaults down below the transaction would also be recorded. As a final check, a portion of the original ticket stayed with control. Until confirmation was made that the security had been deposited in the appropriate account in the vault, or had been received by the proper outside institution, holdover control showed the item as outstanding business. Audits every few days pinpointed errors or discrepancies. Frequency of such audits had actually increased in 1969.

It was not a haphazard system of accounts. While the $125-a-week clerks responsible for the securities may have thought the work simple paper shuffling, officials at Morgan Guaranty—from such juniors as Ronald Duffy up through the more exalted executives who dined on superb lemon sole in the company mess—were always aware of the value of the securities. In fact, Morgan Guaranty had discovered during the summer of 1969 a shortage of $4,000 and as a result more stringent controls had been instituted.

But the safeguards of 1969 were not thief-proof. At this stage of U.S. finance, everyone accepted the necessity for the physical existence of securities. The vast bulk of transactions demanded the movement of a paper instrument from point A to point B and often to go even that short distance, the paper actually had to travel physically through C, D, and E before it could get to B. Brokerage houses and banks serving as custodians and managers, while also trading on their own, began to choke on paper during the go-go years of the stock market. In the offices of firms like the Morgan Guaranty Trust, the piles of securities grew higher and higher, and the people responsible for keeping track of the documents fell further and further behind in their work. In some instances people used short cuts, eliminating steps instituted for safety purposes, thereby opening up the opportunities for theft. More often than not, however, the volume of paper and the frantic tries to keep it circulating properly led to human errors, misfiling, mismailing, and mislabeling.

As Ronald Duffy remembered it, on the Monday following the Met win, the regular audit of the proof cage at the securities clearance department indicated that $5,000,000 in Treasury bills were unaccounted for. "That kind of thing happened almost daily then," said Duffy. "It wasn't uncommon to be asked for delivery of something and find it wasn't in the vault. You'd go back to the correspondent bank and with a little bit of egg on your face, you'd ask where is this stuff supposed to be coming from, and it would turn out to be from another bank or a brokerage house or a dealer and still be in our incoming section. When the auditor said the stuff was missing, I figured just another pain in the ass. The missing securities were 4/2 and 4/9 bills [maturity dates were April 2 and 9] and had arrived the day before on a regular incoming ticket. That was probably where they were. We went to incoming and went through the containers piled with securities, we pulled every truck apart, and went item by item, piece by piece, examined and re-examined the stuff for a day."

Ronald Duffy and his cohorts turned their attention to other possible explanations for the missing securities. "We've had piggy-back deliveries before," he said, "where a piece became hooked to another and was sent to a customer. We checked with all of our deliveries [hundreds of pieces mailed or hand delivered] to locate the bills." While this search was carried on, the auditors went over the referral sheets in an attempt to help trace the missing pieces. To the shock of everyone, the total in missing treasury bills amounted to $13,194,000.

The hunt took on a grimmer look. Morgan Guaranty Trust employees, under supervision and wearing protective gloves, began a systematic inspection of the trash collections for the building. All refuse in the building was and still is bagged and tagged according to its origins at Morgan Guaranty Trust. It is then stored for a number of days just in case securities accidentally fall into a wastepaper basket or a disgruntled clerk dumps them. "We have found securities that were thrown out," said Duffy. "But this time it was nothing—paper, used Kotex, torn pantyhose but no Treasury bills.

"After the second or third day of looking I began to get nervous. I can remember pulling apart radiators, pulling the drawers from desks out, but still nothing. In all my years in the security business, however, it just didn't enter my mind that they might be stolen."

On Wednesday, October 22, two days after the search began, the security clearance section passed the word to top executives about the problem. When the missing securities still could not be located after another day's search that seemed to exhaust the possibilities, Eugene Golden, a vice president in charge of security for the Morgan Guaranty Trust, telephoned the New York City Police Department's Bond and Forgery Squad which was housed in the Old Slip police stationhouse.

An affinity between New York's financial district and the city's police department dates back almost one hundred years. As the first head of the department's Detective Squad, Inspector Thomas Byrnes quickly won the favor of Wall Street by setting up an office on Wall Street to keep the neighborhood clear of thieves, pickpockets, and hoodlums. The stock exchange was so grateful that it gave Byrnes and his men free office space in its building, and furthermore Mrs. Byrnes profited to the extent of a stock portfolio worth an estimated $250,000 when the great detective was forced to retire because of corruption in the force.

Somewhere along the line, that close relationship between the Wall Street community and the police had fallen away until the calls concerning thefts in the financial district were routinely handled by whatever detective happened to be available. Until the 1960s such an arrangement was more or less satisfactory. The kinds of crime that afflicted the Wall Street area were the ordinary run of store holdups and robberies of messengers in the streets. The bandits in these cases were interested in cash not securities. In fact, said a veteran detective who worked in the field until 1973, "Burglars doing a job, who had to stay put for a period while a watchman was in the vicinity, or who didn't want to walk away while the safe was being opened and possibly be cheated on the split, would take a dump on the floor. They actually wiped themselves using Treasury bills and other securities."

The go-go years of Wall Street, which vastly expanded the commerce in paper instruments and the inability of the financial community to maintain strict control over the paper, opened up a bright new avenue for investment by organized crime. Bonds and stocks no longer served as toilet paper. After a series of security thefts, the New York City Police Department, in 1966, established the Bond and Forgery Squad located in the Old Slip stationhouse, along with the command for the Narcotics Division. The new unit consisted of five detectives chosen from various squads around the city and was headed by Sgt. Thomas Dolan, Brooklyn-born, soft-spoken, with an Irish choirboy face. "We commandeered a room, a filing cabinet, and a desk, but this was a whole new area for all of us," remembered Dolan of the unit's beginnings. "We had to learn the nomenclature of the business. Merrill Lynch led us by the hand and showed us. We kept going back, really by a process of osmosis, finding out how the securities business operated. There was no time for a leisurely education through courses at some school. We were investigating thefts almost immediately after we were created."

It was Tom Dolan who took the telephone call from Eugene Golden at Morgan Guaranty Trust on October 23. "We showed up with sixty percent of our force," said Dolan. That meant himself, and detectives Benjamin (Dusty) Rhoades and Joseph Leahy. On the telephone Eugene Golden only reported that some securities were missing. The Bond and Forgery detectives thought it was a routine case but said Joe Leahy, "It turned out to be some little hot potato."

Technically, the theft of the securities qualified as a federal offense which meant that the FBI was obligated to enter the case as well as the New York City cops. Possibly because the bank was still hopeful that the missing items would show up without messy publicity, the investigation started low key, with the Bond and Forgery Squad first on the scene.

"We set up the plans for the work flow initially," said

Tom Dolan. "We tried to find out exactly how the work came into the area, then trace it through the system to determine the last point where the stuff was actually seen. There were maybe half a dozen steps in its passage where it stopped at somebody's desk. We determined that it had cleared every step except the last, the trip to the vault. The last man to work on it remembered that when he finished, he put it on a long table from where it was to go on to the vault.

"Then we got the lists of the names of everybody employed, the four hundred people in the departments that handle securities, and the other seven hundred who had access to the area."

After Dolan and company went through this routine for a day, the FBI was at last also notified. "We were there until after seven o'clock the first night," recalled Joe Leahy, a dapper, strapping, gray-haired man who looks like the prototype of a New York City detective. Initially, as the New York police struggled with 1,100 potential suspects, they were aided by a single FBI agent.

When Morgan executive vice president in charge of operations Henry Rohlf learned about the pace of the investigation, he turned banker choleric. "I think he called J. Edgar Hoover direct and asked him what the hell was going on," said Leahy. "We had two hundred of them working on the case almost immediately." Tom Dolan puts the number of FBI people at seventy-five. "They took over a whole floor on the bank and started interviewing people." Rohlf, perhaps with the benignity manufactured by the passage of time, deprecated his role in stepping up the pace.

While the search for the Treasury bills approached its peak intensity, Morgan Guaranty took the steps necessary to prevent losses. Discovery of the amount of loss in the case of Treasury bills was not the same as if the bank came

up short of one hundred shares of American Telephone
and Telegraph owned by A. G. Bell. Treasury bills carry
only serial numbers; no proprietary names distinguish one
certificate from another. In addition, the records of internal
movement of Treasury bills at Morgan Guaranty dealt only
in terms of denominations. The tickets on every order—
maybe 2,500 daily, some of which involved hundreds of
items—had to be retrieved to determine by process of
elimination which serial numbers were actually missing.
This was a job for Ronald Duffy and his aides. Nor could
the search be limited to a single day; the bills could have
been lost on any of six or seven days.

With the numbers and denominations sorted out,
Morgan Guaranty Trust notified the New York Stock
Clearing Association, the twelve Federal Reserve banks,
the two hundred thirty largest commercial banks in the
U.S., Interpol, and R. L. Polk & Co., a publisher of bank
materials that permits clients to use its mailing list, which
covers every bank in the U.S. including all branch offices
plus the gamut of international financial institutions.

Morgan Guaranty sent out a mailing to the Polk list. The letter using both sides of a single sheet, read (See pages 19–20):

With the financial community being notified of the loss,
Morgan Guaranty Trust also faced the unhappy prospect of
going public. "Once I knew the stuff was stolen," said
Henry Rohlf in retrospect, "it was darn disturbing. It was a
dubious distinction to have the largest theft to date. I
guess I felt like Nixon. We had a summit meeting, all the
brass. The attorneys made up a statement which we
handed to the press. Here it is, we said. We didn't try to
hide anything and we avoided what could have been disastrous. The press really didn't make much of the matter."

Rohlf is correct that the newspapers played the story on
page one for only a day and then buried the followup

IMPORTANT NOTICE TO BANKERS AND BROKERS LOST SECURITIES

October 28, 1969

Dear Sir:

Please take notice that between October 14 and 16, 1969 the U. S. Treasury Bills listed on the reverse side hereof were lost.

The Treasury Department and the various Federal Reserve Banks have been notified.

We are advising you of this fact so that you may alert your staff against purchasing any of these securities or accepting them as collateral for loans.

Should any of these Bills be presented to you, please notify your local Police Department, the F.B.I. and the undersigned bank.

MORGAN GUARANTY TRUST COMPANY
OF NEW YORK

23 Wall Street
New York, N. Y.   10015

Telephones: 212 425 2323 ext. 2964
3069
2489

LIST OF LOST SECURITIES

FACE AMOUNT	IDENTIFYING NUMBER
U.S. TREASURY BILLS DUE APRIL 2, 1970	
$1,000,000. each	222803 through 807
U.S. TREASURY BILLS DUE APRIL 9, 1970	
$1,000,000.	226813
500,000. each	104504 and 505
500,000.	104540
100,000. each	1017011 through 020
100,000. each	1017029 through 038
100,000. each	1017054 through 058
100,000.	1017351
100,000. each	1017699 through 703
100,000. each	1017752 through 759
100,000.	1017821
100,000. each	1017837 and 838
100,000. each	1017845 through 848
100,000. each	1017965 and 966
100,000. each	1020218 through 221
50,000. each	478333 through 340
50,000.	479279
10,000. each	3157915 through 918
1,000. each	3181668 through 671

stories. However, what is surprising is that the initial statement by the bank failed to admit definitely to a theft. Morgan Guaranty only announced that the securities were missing. A day later an FBI spokesman remarked that they were considered stolen but the possible reaction was perhaps blunted by the low-key behavior of the bank officials. It is noteworthy that the memorandum that used the mailing lists of R. L. Polk & Co. spoke of the Treasury bills as "lost" rather than stolen.

Both the financial community and the public were now advised of the caper. However, at least eight days passed from the date of theft to the initial notifications and the date on the circular letter is October 28. Given the uncertainty of the mails, as much as two weeks may have elapsed before word reached some institutions or private investors. The delay would be costly.

III

The Caper Chase

Leaving the premises of the Morgan Guaranty Trust with the seventy-eight pieces totaling $13,194,000 offered no challenge to The Person. That amount of paper could have been tucked into a bra, occasioning no notice except a slightly enhanced bust, squirreled away in the waistband of pantyhose or beneath a shirt, tucked into a jacket pocket, carried out in a plain manila envelope, or in a conventional attaché case.

Stealing the Treasury bills had actually been quite simple. The trick would be to convert these paper instruments into untraceable dollars without apprehension. The Person was not an individual intimately connected with organized crime, but The Person had to know somebody with entry. Only organized crime has the capacity to move hot paper swiftly enough to cash in. To the detectives working on the case, the most significant indication of the amateur quality of the theft was the selection of six $1,000,000 notes. The degree of fiduciary concern with the title to a security is directly proportional to size of the piece, which is the extent of liability for anyone stuck with an illegal item. Easiest to pass would be the $1,000 and $10,000 notes but The Person, acting in possibly unprofessional haste, had apparently grabbed what was available at the time. The only countertheory came from Morgan Guaranty officials. They maintained that the suggestion of a connection with the World Series commotion was fanciful and that the brigand originally took the six $1,000,000 notes and then came back for more on a second day and seized the additional amounts after being informed that the big bills would be too difficult to move.

The prevailing price for stolen securities that have not been listed as hot is a minimum of 10 points. The underworld in its appreciation of the values of the world of big finance long ago adopted the language of the trade and discussions between Mafia soldiers with a vocational school education will be sprinkled with knowing references to points. (The point system is based upon a figure of 100 and the points amount to a percentage.) In the matter of the Morgan Guaranty Trust, the 10 points meant roughly $1,300,000, although considering the size of the haul there may have been a considerable downward adjustment. One theory indeed saw The Person as "just a schmuck who grabbed what he could to wipe out a gambling debt. He didn't clear a nickel for himself."

What seems certain is that The Person dumped the paper in toto upon an individual connected to organized crime. The bills passed through a chain of interested parties and then to a fence. The dealer in stolen items needed enough capital to put a big chunk of cash up front, even for a buy at the normal large discount. The fence also had to have knowledge of the right people who would be able to market the T bills.

There are fences who specialize in consumer goods,

others who handle building materials, and then there are those whose profession is traffic in unlawfully obtained securities. Two of the biggest operators in the hot paper game on the East Coast in the 1960s were Jacob Maislich, a.k.a. Jack Mace, a.k.a. Shotgun Jake, and Arthur Tortorello, a.k.a. Artie Todd to friends and acquaintances and business associates. In his forties, Tortorello had affiliations with the Mafia family of Carlo Gambino, while Maislich, a gray-haired man in his late fifties, apparently extended most-favored-nation status to any of the petty duchies of the organized-crime empire.

Before the letters through R. L. Polk, the notifications to the Federal Reserve banks, and the various communications by other institutions had been fully transmitted, some of the loot from the Morgan Guaranty Trust Company had already sped from The Person through echelons of organized crime to a fence and back out to the market for disposal. These items were negotiated before any of the T bills' numbers had been registered as hot, and there was no way to establish that the possessor knew he had stolen goods. They would be the liability of Morgan Guaranty Trust, or more accurately the bank's insurers. "Innocent holders in due course," as they are called, cashed better than $700,000 worth of the missing bills by April 9, 1970, when the last of the notes reached maturity. The innocent holders in due course were all financial institutions that had accepted the bills for redemption or collateral on loans. The organizations, using the customary but superficial proofs of ownership required by banks and not finding the bills on any hot list, had accepted the first offerings as bona fide.

Trade in stolen securities involves more than attempts to cash bonds or notes before the banks learn they are stolen. One of the most common uses of hot paper is as collateral.

"They put the bills in for loans," said a detective on New York's Bond and Forgery Squad. "The bank does not publish the description of the collateral and only runs a check against any lists of known stolen bills. Of course the bank makes the individual sign that he owns the paper and may even ask for some proof of ownership. But that's not difficult to falsify. In addition, organized crime has connections in banks. They may have some executive over a barrel, gambling debts, women, or anything. He puts the stuff in for collateral on a loan or for something like a letter of credit, and approves the individual as being the owner in due course of the collateral. Now the perpetrator has the use of bank money or the letter of credit for a period up to the maturity date of the bond. Organized crime can take a $500,000 treasury bill, use it as collateral for $350,000, put that money to work in the street for shylocking. The interest can be 20 percent, per week. After a couple of months' use of the bank's $350,000, the loan shark's operation has earned a profit of several hundred thousand dollars. Then the loan's paid off, the Treasury bill returned, and if they don't sell it off to some idiot who thinks he can still use it, they can burn it and the thing can never be traced to them."

Stolen Treasury bills have also served as backing for phony stock ventures or as proof of an individual's fiscal responsibility in a private corporation or partnership. And there are always marks who are greedy enough to put up some cash for a hot certificate. They are the people most often arrested in possession of the plunder.

The initial investigations by the FBI and the New York cops had determined that all the missing T bills had passed through every step in processing and were awaiting shipment to the subterranean vaults of the MGTC when they disappeared. The finding, however, brought the agents no closer to the identify of The Person. It still could have been any of the 1,100 people who could have entered the custody section or who worked there.

In charge of the FBI detail was Special Agent Andrew Watson. An agent for fourteen years, he was a tall bachelor who, unlike some FBI men, enjoyed living in New York. "Andy Watson and I got along very well," said Joe Leahy. "But the feds made a mistake when they picked Watson. His specialty was embezzlement. He was terrific when it came to a question of how somebody cooked the books to take money out of the till. But he was wrong for a job on stolen securities. That's always involved with organized crime and Andy just didn't know the names of the guys in that business. Andy didn't know who he was dealing with; something like Morgan Guaranty, that big a haul, everybody's got some of the shit. And he was a kind of nervous guy, too unsure of himself. One suspect who tried to pass a bill, and whom we grabbed, was about to answer my questions after Andy read him his rights the first time. Then Andy made him listen to his rights a second time. The guy was still ready to talk. Finally Andy gave him his rights a third time and the guy now says, 'I don't want to talk until I see my attorney.' That washed him out. One thing about Andy, he scared hell out of me in New York traffic. He drove like he was in a corn field."

Whatever his defects, Andy Watson knew the drill. The FBI agents and the New York City police began an agonizingly long series of interviews with every employee of Morgan who had access to the area from which the bills were taken. What they were looking for was information on the background of the individual interviewed, plus the standard FBI collection of office gossip that might point toward somebody else's behavior, some closet skeleton that would be a motive for the theft.

While Watson and company dug into the lives of the employees, other agents prowled the Miami, Florida, area. A few weeks earlier, Treasury bills taken from a Wall Street firm had surfaced in Miami and the Florida Gold Coast had traditionally been a popular territory for high rollers who dealt in illegitimate high finance. Agents went from bank to bank personally to alert auditors and head tellers to be on the watch for the bills.

They eagerly checked out a lead. An employee of Morgan Guaranty had arrived in Miami shortly after the robbery. His movements were traced through a Hertz car rental and hotel registration. Agents poured over the Hertz receipt showing the man had driven the car ninety-two miles and they went through the checkout slips at the hotel seeking names. The gossamer lead blew away as nothing substantial appeared.

A brief flurry in New York centered on another worker who had managed to sign himself out at the register in the custody section of the bank on one of the nights in question but whose name did not appear in the signout book in the lobby of the building. That too failed to open up any avenues of exploration. The agents continued to look for gamblers, people in hock to loan sharks, secret swingers, ex-convicts, and people with any other signs of what they considered a weakness.

On another front, there was the question of insurance for the thefts. Morgan was covered by a policy for $6,000,000 with Chubb & Son, the next $3,000,000 was the responsibility of Continental Casualty, and another $3,000,000 lay on the doorstep of INA (Insurance Company of North America). "When we heard the news," said a Chubb official, "we arranged a meeting within three hours." All was not harmony with the three insurers. The people from Chubb suggested to their colleagues from the other companies that since there would inevitably be protracted litigation in the recovery of some items (based on past experience) legal expenses should be shared. Said a Chubb participant at the meeting, "The reaction, in effect, was the hell with you. We're not even sure of our liability." The question of whether or not there had been a single theft or two separate ones was at first a significant issue. If it were a single action, then the $13,000,000 loss obviously reached all three insurers. However, if it were determined that the losses were broken into $5,000,000 and $8,000,000, then Chubb would be hit for all of the first and $6,000,000 on the second in accord with its liability. Continental would only be stuck for something over $2,000,000 while INA would be home free. That presupposed that there would be no recovery at all. As it developed, the insurance loss totaled only in the neighborhood of $700,000 and the question did not need resolution.

While the FBI plodded through its search, The Person continued to evade discovery, the insurance companies studied their contracts, and the market in stolen securities churned.

IV

The Marvins

The T bills strolled out of Morgan Guaranty Trust on the afternoon of October 16. By the twenty-fourth of the month, the worker ants of the FBI, augmented by the Bond and Forgery Squad representatives, were on the case. They swarmed over the premises to poke into every cranny in the lives of the 1,100 suspects.

The Person had played the lead in the first scene of the drama. But the seventy-eight pieces taken from the bank were only that—pieces of paper. They would become real money only after they were negotiated. This called for some backstage business, and the real action shifted away from the building at the corner of Broad and Wall streets.

A whole new cast of characters trooped onto the stage. The dramatis personae included some genuine wise guys, bona fide members of organized crime. Alongside of them swam their remoras, the fringe people who hung around to pick up morsels dropped by the bigger fishes. High binders with a laundry list of fraudulent security operations in their history assembled to play roles. A covey of businessmen—some quite respectable, some less so—lawyers, accountants, innocent dupes, hustlers, young men on the make, old-timers out for a last big score—many tinged with a larcenous twist—joined the show. Bankers, numerous lawmen, assorted legal counselors popped in and out as spear carriers. No single individual dominated the action; the principal interest was the seventy-eight pieces. Having left the normal business confines, those pieces had become endowed with a new kind of life, like rural innocents who suddenly discover the city. For a maximum of six months, these seventy-eight pieces of paper would dictate the behavior of hundreds of humans. Many would be caught up in frantic games of hide, seek, prosecute, and defend. The bills would fascinate the best and worst minds of the criminal kingdom and seduce hitherto virtuous citizens into monumental transgressions. At the end of six months, the bills would be dead, leaving behind a handful of people who exploited them, a larger number whose lives had been blighted by contact. The legacy of the dead or, more correctly, retired paper would be the lessons of history. Banks and brokerage houses could either discover how to avoid losses or they could ignore the experience and thereby invite further raids on their property.

On October 20, 1969, the day Morgan Guaranty Trust employees first noticed some incongruity in their accounts, FBI agent Robert Sheehan in the Boston offices of the Bureau was checking all Treasury bills fed into the Federal Reserve Bank in Boston. Sheehan was on the alert because the government had just discovered a ring of T-bill swindlers operating in the area. He spotted a $100,000 bill marked 1017012A. Sheehan inquired of the National Crime Information Center if the bill was listed as stolen. The answer came back negative. He telephoned the FBI in New York and the U.S. Treasury in Washington but the note still came out clean. It was not a number on any hot list but Sheehan could see the route taken by the Treasury bill. It had been sent for collection to the New England Merchants National Bank from the Town Bank and Trust in Brookline, Massachusetts, a suburb of Boston. Within a few hours, Sheehan put the arm on the man who had pledged the T bill at Town Bank and Trust for a loan. He was Marvin Karger, a pudgy five-foot-six native of Revere, another Boston suburb. On his arrest, Karger was immediately charged with passing more than $1,600,000 in stolen securities. Later, when Sheehan confirmed that the $100,000 note presented on October 20, had also been the product of the theft from Morgan Guaranty, that too was added to the list of counts against Karger.

Marvin Karger, born in 1933, came from a reasonably well off if not wholly respectable family. The household's income derived directly from business enterprises backed by Marvin Karger's maternal uncle, one Louis Fox. "He was," said Marvin Karger, "a wicked bastard. Louis Fox was the payoff man for the mob in the Boston area. He was the connection between the Mafia and the politicians. He was involved in bookmaking, had a piece of the Wonderland Dog Track [a mob operated enterprise]."

Louis Fox set up a liquor store, then a vending machine business, for Marvin Karger's father to operate. Marvin and his brother attended the local schools, Tilton Prep and Revere High School, but never for a moment was Marvin Karger allowed to forget who was the patriarch of the family. "If Louis Fox came to the house, I would have to stay in my room and be available if he wanted anything. When he came for a meal, the finest silver and china went on the table along with the best food. If I took a can of peaches and sour cream for myself, my mother would find the can in the garbage and she'd hit me for indulging myself. I took to eating from the cans on the back porch and then I'd throw the cans over the fence. The way they kowtowed to Louis Fox, kissed his ass, made me sick."

Marvin Karger's distress took two forms; he became a compulsive eater. At the time Bob Sheehan arrested Karger he hung 270 pounds on his five-foot-six frame. He ballooned into that shape as he entered manhood. In addition, by age 18 he was what he called "a degenerate gambler."

It was the horses that Marvin Karger backed, and more often than not, slow horses. By the time he was 18, he was stealing from his household to cover his bets at the track and with bookmakers. The concerned family institutionalized the young gambler in Greenlawn, a private sanitarium in Ossining, New York (home also of the more famed hostel for the wayward, Sing Sing prison). "The psychiatrist said my trouble came from an unsettled home-life," explained Karger. "My brother became screwed up too. He quit school after the seventh grade. My therapy included electroshock, and the usual run of counseling. While I was at Greenlawn I went to the local high school, had dates, even played goalie for the hockey team. The doctor said I'd do all right if I stayed away from my family, but when I finished high school I went back to Revere."

There was a respite while Karger served in the army from 1954 to 1957. He pulled peaceful duty in Korea. Honorably discharged, Karger rolled with the great continental tilt to California. "There I met the girl who became my wife and took a shipping clerk's job in a hosiery distributor. My gambling at this stage was minimal. After I got to know some of the manufacturers I went into business for myself. I did all right until there was a long dock strike. Most of my stuff was imported, the orders were all canceled and I went broke."

Bankrupt, Marvin Karger headed straight back to the

family bosom. "Home is the place they have to take you in," said Robert Frost in "The Hired Man"; but the hired man dies. And for Marvin Karger the milk of the family bosom was a kind of poison.

Working for his father at $90 a week, Marvin Karger, father of three, wrestled with vending machines, collected the nickels, dimes, and quarters. His old infection, gambling, erupted with renewed fury. He continued to be a poor judge of horseflesh and although he hustled at everything possible, Karger worked himself up to an $8,000 debt with the shylocks. "I'd write bad checks, and then I'd cover the bad check with an even bigger check. I had a respectable businessman who would endorse the backs of the checks; he trusted me and never even looked to see the size of the amounts. But finally when I wrote one for $8,000 I was indicted. My father made the check good and I received two years' probation."

The affair caused Karger to seek employment away from his father. He became a salesman for a company that manufactured vending machines. "It was owned by an old man from West Virginia, James MacGregor. He came to Massachusetts, met me, liked the way I operated and he backed me in my own vending machine company." MacGregor dreamed of beverage and candy machines on every high pedestrian traffic corner in Boston. He pushed Karger into a financial disaster. "There wasn't enough business to pay off the machines which I got from MacGregor on a loan from his company. His company put pressure on me to pay off the $50,000 advanced because they had to pay their loans from the West Virginia bank. Of course you know who owned that bank, James MacGregor. He was such a dignified gentleman, didn't swear, didn't drink, didn't smoke, but could he tuck it to you!" Karger wound up broke again.

"I grabbed anything to make a buck to support my family. I was so desperate that I hustled hot goods. One Sunday, in March of 1969, I took my daughter to breakfast at a delicatessen in Newton [another Boston suburb], called Arnold's. The eggs for my daughter came cold. I complained and the owner said, 'You don't like it, buy the joint.' I said, 'How much?' He said, 'Forty thousand,' and I said, 'Sold.' " Amid the egg-crusted plates of the breakfast, Marvin Karger now used $600 in his wallet to secure the contract. It was agreed that the total down payment would be $5,000 with the rest taken as a mortgage. Karger raised the additional cash from vending machine concessionaires, always available to advance money in return for the right to install their own devices. Arnold's became "The Onion Roll" and as a delicatessen restaurant it produced a decent income, if one did not have Marvin Karger's unscratchable itch to invest in horses.

"In June, I got a call from Vinnie Teresa. I hadn't seen him in maybe a year. He was a loudmouth slob, a pig. He hung around with a colored girl; nobody really trusted him. There were places in Boston, restaurants where the wise guys hung out and they wouldn't let Teresa into the places because they didn't trust him. Teresa's made a big thing of himself, number-three man in the Mafia in New England. He was nothing but a slob. Vinnie said, 'Come on down and see me.' He was with another fellow, and they showed me $34,000 in Treasury notes. They said they were legit. Teresa said he got them from a bookmaker who took them in payment from a client. They wanted to know if I could sell them."

Teresa, at 320 pounds, outweighed Karger by a flabby 50, but he had a much richer history. He had been a shylock, hijacker, gambler, dealer in hot cars, and according to him a heavyweight in the stolen securities trade. He had, of course, lied to Marvin Karger. Several days before he renewed his acquaintance, Teresa was holding forth at his principal place of business, the Esquire Sportsmen's Club in a Boston office suite, when a call came in from New York City. The voice identified itself as Jack Mace, a.k.a. Jacob Maislich. Mace was known equally well to both the FBI and organized crime as one of the most active fences on the East Coast. He brokered a wide variety of merchandise, from credit cards through securities, using a coin shop in Manhattan as his major front.

"Take this number down and call me back from a pay phone," Mace instructed Teresa. The proprietor of the Esquire Sportsmen's Club obliged, right in his office. For convenience, the telephone company had installed a pay phone. The convenience for Teresa and friends was that, while any phone line (including the pay phone) on their premises was still subject to a tap, the telephone company only kept records of toll calls made on ordinary business telephones. Coin installations demanded the payment before the parties were connected. Therefore Ma Bell retained no embarrassing records for the edification of the FBI.

Mace informed Teresa that he had some U.S. Treasury bills. They were taken out of the company a few days ago. There was no heat on them and their face value was $34,000. To confirm the substance of Jack Mace's offering, he put on the wire a colleague, Arthur Tortorello, a.k.a. Artie Todd, and like Mace a middleman in the traffic of stolen goods. "I just got these things a couple of nights ago," said Arthur Tortorello. "They are beautiful. They are ice cold. They've got a maturity date in August. There should be no trouble moving these things at all."

Tortorello asked for 25 points, finally Teresa bargained him down to 20 points. Tortorello had enough faith in his merchandise to offer the bills to Teresa on credit. There was to be no payment up front. The fence was willing to wait seven to ten days for his approximately $6,500.

Because Teresa was recuperating from an auto accident, he dispatched Vincent Chiodi and John Cefalo, one-time partners in a doughnut shop in East Boston, to pick up the paper. Teresa wanted the messenger boys to fly to New York, but they preferred the safety of an automobile. They drove to New York City that afternoon. In front of Jack Dempsey's restaurant—the agreed upon rendezvous point—"a short fat guy with a crew cut, blue eyes" approached the car with the two emissaries. "Are you Vincent Chiodi?"

The passenger admitted to his identity. The sidewalk envoy passed an envelope. "Bring these right back to Boston and give them to Teresa." The Bostonians headed north with the Treasury bills. Somewhere en route Cefalo pulled the car off the highway and the two men refreshed themselves with a nap. At 7:30 A.M. they arrived at Teresa's home in Revere, Massachusetts, and delivered the cargo. Until he could find a way to sell the bills, Teresa stashed them behind a plastic block in the ceiling of his office.

His first choice to dispose of the hot paper, he subsequently testified, was not Marvin Karger but one Jerry Myers, who ran a local boatyard. Myers at the time was on a course toward the shoals of financial insolvency. Teresa gave Myers the bills to cash at the New England Merchants National Bank. The boatyard man fretted over the deal; Teresa had not informed him of the origins of the securities but Myers had caught a whiff of larceny in the air. In fact, he'd been questioned by FBI men on his friend Teresa. He went to the bank, accompanied by Teresa's assistant, Joan Harvey, an attractive woman in her late twenties. Joan Harvey, besides serving as a gracious appurtenance to his suite of offices, was someone whom Teresa trusted completely.

Jerry Myers engaged an officer of the bank in a brief

conversation and then reported to Teresa that his man would advise Myers of the procedure required by New England Merchants National Bank. A day or so later, Myers returned to Teresa with the Treasury bills to report that the bank didn't want to participate in the transaction. "I could see he was a nervous wreck," said Teresa of Myers. "I told him that I thought he didn't really try."

Teresa was absolutely correct. For Myers, worried about the legality of the operation, had never even asked the bank to negotiate the bills. Instead, he simply asked the banker to hold the securities overnight for him. The purpose of Myers' charade was to placate Teresa, who on occasion displayed the temper of a bull rhino in the rutting season.

At one period of his life Teresa had owned a yacht. He had become acquainted with Marvin Karger while the latter managed a cocktail lounge near the boatyard. Teresa knew all about Karger's background of Uncle Louis Fox and the nephew's gambling habit. He thus arranged to meet with Karger at The Onion Roll after Myers opted out of the plot.

Teresa has insisted that he kept nothing back from Karger. "I went on to explain to him that there was a hot list in banks and brokerage houses and if he brought them to a lawyer, or a bank, got a loan of 70 or 80 percent the only thing is whatever lawyer or bank that you go to, you must know who you are doing business with—and you must tell him these things are stolen or else they will kick back on you later."

Karger called his lawyer, Philip Allen. "I asked him to check them out every possible way. When he reported to me that the bills were okay as far as anyone could see, I went to the Town Bank and Trust." The actual mechanism for selling the paper was through a demand promissory note for $26,000 from Philip Allen and his office associate,

Joseph Lee, a real estate investor. The T bills served as collateral. The participants divided up the initial proceeds; Marvin Karger kept $4,000 to split with Lee and Allen. Cefalo and Chiodi brought an envelope with $22,000 to Teresa, who rewarded the messengers with three big ones each. He gave Joan Harvey $800, sent $4,500 to Jack Mace and Arthur Tortorello, and kept $10,000 for himself. A few days later, Town Bank and Trust sold the T bills to liquidate the promissory note and that produced another $5,000 which served to wipe out the last indebtedness to the New York fences and spread a little more joy to everyone. Karger believed that his total on the transaction was between $2,000 and $3,000 and that Lee and Allen might have received as much as $5,000. The use of demand notes rather than loans for a period of time—30, 60, or 90 days—permitted Town Bank to liquidate the obligation whenever it wished to.

Vincent Teresa was not around to savor further the pleasures the deal brought. Earlier in the month he had been convicted by a Baltimore jury of negotiating stolen Treasury bills and he was also on trial for auto theft in Massachusetts.

However, the success of the Town Bank and Trust venture indicated to Teresa's associates that they had opened up a highway paved with gold. "A month later," said Karger, "two people friendly with Teresa gave me the same story about a bookmaker settling up with Treasury notes. I knew it was bullshit but nothing happened the first time so I started to go. I didn't try to check anything out anymore." Nor did anyone else apparently.

"I met with three or four different guys," Karger said, "who would bring the notes to me. One of them was Teresa's partner Joseph Lamattina. Sometimes it was at The Onion Roll, other occasions elsewhere. I would call the bank officer at 7:30 in the morning and say I'm coming in with another Treasury bill. Would you have $35,000 or $50,000 ready for me. And I'd get the money within minutes after I came there. Sometimes Allen and Lee went with me to the bank to sign the notes, sometimes they came in later. I'd call them up and say, 'I have some Marvins,' and they'd come running.

"I used anything to haul away the cash, ladies' overnight cases, brief cases. One time I picked up $70,000 and all they had were five-dollar bills. Do you know what a pile $70,000 in five-dollar bills is? I left the bank with the money in two big shopping bags. On the sides of the bags it said something like, 'Come back and see us again.' As I got to the door, I turned and yelled, 'I'll be happy to come back and see you again.'

"I didn't have time to think about getting caught. I was so goddam over my head in gambling debts and I'd already cashed the one piece, what difference would it make if I did more of the same thing? When you're making that kind of money, $15,000 to $20,000 a week, you lose any conception of what you're doing.

"Actually, I was cheated. The people who brought the stuff to me kept telling me they paid 50 percent of the face value for the bills. Actually, they put up 18 to 22 percent I found out later. My share should have been much bigger. On a $100,000 note the guy would claim he had paid $50,000 for it. We might clear $30,000 above that, of which I would get to keep $15,000 and he'd say all he was taking was the other $15,000. What was left (perhaps $12,000 to $15,000) went to the bank and to Lee and Allen. But my man wasn't getting just $15,000. He was getting more than half of that $50,000 that he said the bill cost. I should have had a share of that."

Between June and October 20, 1969, Marvin Karger toted Treasury bills to the Town Bank and Trust on sixteen separate occasions and once to another local institution, the Garden City Bank. Each time the bills were pledged to back promissory notes issued in the names of Philip Allen and Joseph Lee. The total amount in Treasury bills negotiated by Marvin Karger came to $1,714,000. Only the last $100,000 item belonged to Morgan Guaranty Trust; the others came from the vaults of such organizations as MacDonald & Co., G. H. Walker brokerage houses, and Marine Midland Bank, all in New York City.

"I probably made about $250,000," says Karger. "I blew it all on the horses. Lee and Allen must have gotten $400,000. The promissory notes were never for the full value of the bills. We'd borrow maybe $88,000 on a $100,000 note. When the bank would sell the bill three or four days after they issued the promissory note, the last $5,000 to $7,000 would be kept by Lee and Allen. Normal commission for a broker is supposed to be one percent, so they did very well."

Whether Vincent Teresa, who had turned cooperative with authorities, tipped off the feds to the Town Bank and Trust capers or some other source fingered the scenario with Marvin Karger as the lead actor is unclear. But after special agent Sheehan arrested Karger, Vincent Teresa provided the government with the names of others he said were involved. Two separate cases were brought; one against Karger and another against Jack Mace, Arthur Tortorello, Vincent Chiodi, John Cefalo, Joseph Lamattina (a.k.a. Joe Black), and Joan Harvey. Vincent Teresa was scheduled to be a prime witness against all of the defendants. The Joint Strike Force, the special Justice Department unit created to push prosecution of organized crime, did not lodge complaints against Joseph Lee and Philip Allen.

Marvin Karger, however, pleaded guilty to all eighteen counts against him. The judge at the trial then asked if Karger would cooperate against others involved. "Are you free or not free to disclose their identity?" The guilty man answered no. And then continued, "I do not fear for my safety. I went into this thing with my eyes open, not closed, and I feel as though it's a responsibility on my part that I was not deceived by people."

Although his client had not cooperated with the feds in the continuing investigation, defense lawyer Joseph Oteri negotiated with the prosecution to secure a recommendation for a five-year term. When it came time to sentence Marvin Karger, the U.S. Attorney duly made his recommendation for a five-year sentence. The judge ignored the suggestion and ordered Marvin Karger to serve a total of twelve years, the stiffest penalty anyone involved in the entire case received.

While Karger was packed off to various federal penitentiaries, the other principals faced their days before their peers. During the trials of various individuals implicated in the Marvins, Vincent Teresa appeared as a star prosecution witness. He explained, out of court, that he became a tale spinner because Joe Black, who ran off to Sicily, cheated him of his rightful share of more than $1,700,000 in cashed Marvins. (Joseph Lamattina, an associate of Teresa's who had an even sleazier reputation for trustworthiness than his partner, fled the country. Lamattina had been one of the people who brought T bills to Karger after Teresa was locked up. There is some speculation that his disappearance is due equally to fear of prosecution and retribution by the other outlaws. He apparently stiffed the crime fraternity on his last delivery, the $100,000 Treasury bill from Morgan Guaranty. Teresa claimed that since he had devised the scheme, even though he was in the federal penitentiary, he should have received compensation from the sales of the securities.)

On the basis of Vincent Teresa's testimony, Jack Mace was found guilty, as was John Cefalo; Vincent Chiodi pleaded guilty. Arthur Tortorello and Joan Harvey were acquitted. Tortorello's acquittal in the Town Bank and Trust operation only temporarily cooled the hot breath of the feds pursuing him. Possibly because they had been tipped to his role by Teresa or because other sources of information had identified Tortorello as a major trafficker in illegal securities, the offices in which he operated were bugged, legally, by the FBI. The tapes, introduced in a later case against the fence, offer the flavor of big-time criminal finance.

For example, Tortorello held a long conversation with a man named Fred Hesse, who was also busily engaged in trading pieces that were not his to sell.

Hesse opened up: "Now, ah, oh, Howie, just called me. He is looking to buy, he calls them LCs [letters of credit] and he, and he is, he's telling me twenty-five million out of Chase, I've got a market for fifteen of the, or out of Manufacturers or something and he's got a market for fifteen million of them. . . ."

Hesse related how he chose to be coy. "So I just play Dicky the Dunce about . . ." "On this end," Tortorello interjected, "up here, we were speaking about LCs. . . . We were speaking about LCs and when he called me he said that there's still a market available for LCs? I said let's go see if there are buyers. These are substantial people with ah . . ."

"Very big," finished Tortorello's associate.

The fence continued his sentence, ". . . with several years, with banks. I said is it coming from, 'cause Eddie at that time was indicating insurance companies. I sez coming from the same source, an insurance company. He sez not from overseas. I sez, well, we'll have to read one and get, see what it looks like, see the language on it."

"What they have, they have time CDs, certificates of deposits. Time certificates of deposit on the Bank of Sorge, Sark, which is an island off the coast of England."

The Bank of Sark was a notable paper creation of the financial high binders. Supposedly located in the Guernsey Islands off Normandy, its cashier's checks, letters of credit, and other assets might just as easily have been issued by the Grand Banks off Newfoundland.

Tortorello and Hesse reviewed the maneuvers that changed worthless paper into cash. "Alright," said Tortorello, "assuming he gives you a $100,000 debenture which your guy gets $60,000 [in a loan]—"

Hesse interrupted, "Or gets 70 or gets 80, whatever he gets."

"He would get 50 percent," said the fence.

"Fifty percent of the proceeds of the loan," confirmed Hesse.

"Yeah, of the loan, naturally. And he would have to take care of whatever the case may be." [Meaning the party that filched the debenture.]

"Right," continued Hesse, "and also maybe us. Give us 5 to 10 points."

"How many years does it run, the debenture?" asked Tortorello.

"He says one year, two years, three years. I told him not to run under a year. . . . I told him to run five-year debentures where a year has elapsed, four to go . . . back date them if he has to." The issue of the length of time to maturity on a bond is critical for thieves. Legal precedents in the United States generally hold that a purchaser of a note after its maturity date risks liability. The presumption is that bona fide investors do not buy obligations after they no longer earn interest.

Later during the same conversation came other hints about how things are done.

Hesse remarked, "They did something with Underwriters today. I just got the call before I came here."

Asked Tortorello, "Who's that?"

"Arnold Wells. And the reason he was able to do something he was overdrawn with his bank, $5,000. So the
banker, to get himself off the hook, made a loan to him. So
I got to go over the figures with . . ."

"And all the bank would lend was 30 percent against the
last bid which was like six, seven dollars, that they go. The
bank wouldn't go for more than the thirty." It was clear evidence of collusion by a banker with a securities swindler.

Several exchanges revealed that even in the crook world
of finance not everything goes smoothly.

Hesse explained, "Now the one thing that I'm working
with with Wells, which would be on a new issue. He's got
two shylocks in Jersey that are pushing it out with their
customers, to hock with the banks to get off."

Grumbled Arthur Tortorello, "Actually from what you
tell me whatever the past few weeks have come up, I
haven't seen nothing yet."

"To this moment," agreed Hesse, "I haven't made dime
one . . . everybody busy, running, jumping, dime one
hasn't been made at this moment."

Tortorello asked the whereabouts of an associate. "I
think he's running around like a fart in a wind tunnel in
California," replied the caller.

One colleague complained bitterly to Tortorello about a
problem in court. "I've have more damn trouble with the
damn judge today than I can shake a stick at. . . . He don't
read the goddam law. I'm gonna have to learn him how to
read."

During the many conversations a certain edginess crept
into some of the dialogue. For example, Tortorello voiced
worry over the trustworthiness of some customers to a
chap identified as Harry Levy. "Jack is honorable," pro-

tested Levy. "Jack will take his fucking pants off. What's the matter with you?" (A willingness to bare one's behind was a metaphor for what could be called rock-bottom honesty.)

Tortorello, still not fully convinced, remarked, "It's his associate that knows about—"

Levy broke in. "What are you talking about? Nobody is trying to be honorable with him. He's a thief. What's to be honorable."

At times, the conspirators sensed that there might be eavesdroppers about. They lapsed into Yiddish, talked of the sale of "two restaurants," "cigars," the sale of "fifty-six sweaters," "two hundred bathing suits," or a bit more transparently announced, "The $1.50 item is gone." The tries to conceal the nature of business done by Tortorello and friends proved feeble. Largely through the tapes, he was found guilty of securities fraud and slapped with a five-year sentence, about one year after his colleague Jack Mace received a similar penalty for the Boston Marvins.

Although the criminal trials were over in relatively short order, the Marvins operations left a messy residue of scar tissue. Morgan Guaranty in 1971 filed suit against Karger, Lee, and Allen to recover the approximately $35,000 paid to Karger when he brought the last bill to the Town Bank and Trust. Morgan attached $1,000,000 in real estate that belonged to Lee and Allen. Morgan also asked a summary judgment against Town Bank and Trust for the other $61,293.81 that the Brookline institution retained after it so hastily sold the $100,000 bill to cover the $35,000 promissory note. Town Bank and Trust insisted on retaining the $61,293.81 because it said Marvin Karger might have some legitimate claim on the bill, and the bank wished to be protected against suit from him. Obviously, Marvin Karger, having pleaded guilty to knowledge that the paper he negotiated was stolen, had no claim.

Meanwhile, Town Bank and Trust pursued Lee and Allen in the event that any judgments were entered against the bank for moneys advanced to the pair during the Marvins operations. Finally, Lee and Allen filed a libel case against Morgan Guaranty, because that corporation's petition stated, "Karger knew said bill was stolen and on information and belief, Allen and Lee had reason to know said bill was stolen." Lee and Allen hit both Morgan and Marine Midland, which had used similar language in its petitions, with demands for a million dollars each in libel damages.

In July, 1971, observing no evidence of any possible claim from Karger, Judge Charles Wyznanski abruptly ordered Town Bank and Trust to fork over the more than $61,000 to Morgan Guaranty. But the other matters dragged on until 1974. Lee and Allen refunded the $35,000 to Morgan.

Marvin Karger, meanwhile, spent his time in various federal jails seeking release. He shuttled from the Allenwood minimum-security pen in Lewisburg, Pennsylvania, to Eglin Air Force Base in Florida, where he associated with other minimum-security prisoners. "It was a cowshit place, fifteen hundred cattle," said Karger. At Eglin he tried to advance his education through a program that permitted well-behaved inmates to attend a local junior college. He also asked for the privilege of a communal visit from his wife. Suddenly his right to attend classes was revoked and his request for the communal visit denied. Somebody in the Justice Department or Bureau of Prisons studying his history had decided Karger was insufficiently cooperative to be allowed the privileges. Karger's difficulty lay in the notation, "Associated with the fringes of organized crime" on his dossier.

Joseph Oteri had received $50,000 to plead Marvin Karger guilty and the attorney donated $31,000 of the fee to his client's family. Destitute, Karger obtained court-appointed counsel to file an appeal for a reduction in sentence. The basic legal argument was that the presiding judge should have been advised that the defendant admitted his guilt only as the result of a plea bargain. In some federal districts it has become mandatory to inform the judge that the defendant has admitted his culpability in return for a promise by the prosecution to recommend a lighter sentence. However, in any case, as with Karger, the U.S. Attorney is only empowered to recommend leniency. The plea of guilty is not a guarantee of a short sentence.

In reviewing Marvin Karger's appeal, Judge D. J. Tauro of the First District said, "In this case, the judge asked for the Government's recommendation as well as for its basis [that a guilty plea would save the government the expense and effort of a long and uncertain trial]. He was not told of the plea bargain. The reasons that were given for the recommendation did not even intimate that a plea bargain existed. . . . While the judge was not bound by the Government's recommendation, it is impossible to speculate what effect, if any, knowledge of the plea bargain might have had on the sentence imposed."

Judge Tauro ordered the twelve-year sentence vacated and Karger to be resentenced. In effect, it turned him loose in January, 1975, as the new sentence amounted to time already served. However, the government filed an appeal on this decision.

While this petition for resentencing had inched its way through the courts, Karger appeared before a parole board and achieved a favorable response. He received written notice toward the end of August, 1974, that he would be paroled October 17, 1974. However, on September 30 of that year the Board of Parole rescinded the order for Karger's release.

The Board of Parole accompanied its decision to revoke

the parole with a notice of its reasons: "Your offense is rated as very high severity. You have a salient factor score of 9 [on a scale of 1 to 11, murder of prison guard would be a 1, perfect behavior an 11]. The guidelines established by the Board which consider the above factors indicate a range of 26 to 36 months to be served before release for adult cases with good institutional program performance and adjustment. You have been in custody a total of approximately 48 months. After careful consideration of all relevant factors and information presented, it is found that a decision *outside the guidelines* [my italics] is warranted because of the magnitude of the offense." Additionally, "The Board has new and fuller information on your organized crime activities received September 30, 1974, in a communication from the Criminal Division, Dept. of Justice, Washington, D.C., which caused the Board to conclude that, if released on parole, there would not be a reasonable probability that you would live and remain at liberty without again violating the law."

The "severity" of Karger's offense as an element in the change in parole plans was mystifying. What he had done had never been in doubt or hidden either from the prosecution or the parole board members.

As for his organized crime activities, Marvin Karger was strictly a small-time fringe operator. He was never as close to the larcenous ways of the Mafia as Vincent Teresa was. Conceivably, people in the Justice Department regarded Karger with malice because while he pleaded guilty to the crime he stubbornly refused to cooperate in any deeper investigations into the Marvins. For example, he would not give up the names of those parties who had delivered Treasury bills to him at The Onion Roll and other rendezvous. Actually, the twelve years originally given to Karger smacks of cruel and unusual punishment. Murderers and a host of other violent offenders draw less time than Karger,

whose sentence stands as the heaviest meted out to anyone convicted for a role in the Morgan Guaranty robbery.
(Admittedly, he was charged with many other similar vio-
lations involving other institutions.)

"They stuck it to me," said Karger, "because they
wanted to justify that money spent on Vincent Teresa and
his testimony. He went before the Senate and gave all
those names and none of them pleaded guilty."

The pressure from the Justice Department to keep
Karger tucked away, even though its own representatives
had originally recommended leniency, reflects the standard
coercion employed by the government to encourage anyone connected to organized crime to inform. In Karger's
case, the likelihood is that he could supply a certain
amount of gossip, little substance. What is significant
about Karger's travail with representatives of the Justice
Department is the infinite ways the government can bring
pressure on a target.

The firm of Silverglate, Shapiro, and Gertner undertook
to represent Karger when he contested the parole-board
decision. A U.S. District Court judge agreed the board had
violated its own rules by rescinding the release without an
additional hearing. But instead of ordering the petitioner's
freedom, Judge Garrity only ruled that the board had to
convene again on Karger's application for parole. He was,
naturally, turned down. Silverglate, Shapiro, and Gertner
took this matter to the U.S. Court of Appeals for the First
District. As it stood in 1975 Karger was free. But if the government won its appeal against his resentencing and he
lost his appeal of the parole-board determination, Marvin
Karger would return to prison.

There was very little left of Marvin Karger's former life
when he did secure his uncertain release in January, 1975.
His wife was in the process of obtaining a divorce. "My father died a millionaire and disinherited me. The rest of

the family, my mother and brother, tried to keep me away from his funeral. They never even wrote me a letter while I was in prison. The house my kids lived in is being fore-closed, there's a third mortgage of $17,000 or so on it. I asked my mother to take over the mortgage so my kids could stay there. She said no. It's forbidden to mention my name in her house. My family, money is their whole God. My mother would say, 'You can never hurt me unless you hurt my pocketbook.' "

A mere butterball of 220 (he was 270 at the time of ar-rest), Karger moved in with an aunt and uncle in Revere. Another relative gave him a job managing a small busi-ness. For the time being at least, Marvin Karger claims to be cured of his interest in horses.

There are some odd aspects to the case of the Marvins. The most obvious question is how could the Town Bank have continued for more than three months to be a party to the operation. Treasury bills are not customarily utilized to serve as collateral for loans by private individuals. They are devices for short-term investment which are either converted into other investments before maturity or often rolled over at maturity. The proceeds are used to pick up new Treasury issues which will earn interest until a satis-factory investment is located. For a delicatessen owner to march into a bank, week in and week out, and borrow large sums of money the way Marvin Karger did suggests carelessness, at best. Nobody at the Town Bank was mind-ing the store.

Neither Joseph Lee nor Philip Allen suffered prosecu-tion. They were not named as co-conspirators. Both of them profited on the loans in the amount of several hundred thousands, more in fact than the feckless Karger was able to blow on horses. Their brokerage fee is in excess of what any normal brokerage firm would charge for negotiating T bills.

As far as Marvin Karger was concerned there was never any question about the naïveté of others who participated. "You have got to be a moron not to know that these things were hot."

The degree to which the Town Bank and Trust was aware of some irregularities in the Marvins business is emphasized by its behavior with the $100,000 bill from Morgan Guaranty tendered by the delicatessen owner on October 20, 1969. On other occasions, the bank waited several days before disposing of the collateral. But in this instance, the bill was put in for collection the very same day that Karger came to borrow the $35,000. The only explanation would seem to be that the Town Bank and Trust—suddenly alerted by FBI Agent Sheehan that its favored customer, Marvin Karger, had used the Town Bank and Trust as a conduit for the negotiation of stolen securities—instantly tried to guard against any loss on its part by selling off the bill which was still not registered as hot.

For that matter, the question of how the FBI discovered the flow of Marvins raises some other questions. The pipeline opened in June of 1969, and while the bills were disposed of nearly every week, nobody traced the source or the traffic pattern followed by these bills for better than three months. Any of the bills that reached maturity during this period would have been presented to the Federal Reserve, which certainly should have been advised that the pieces were stolen. But even if the feds spotted the paper as hot, the trail could still be difficult to track back to the source. Trading in Treasury bills often goes solely by denomination and maturity date, not by serial numbers as well. How was anyone to know that a particular Treasury bill was first presented at the Town Bank and Trust without having passed through several other institutions before it finally arrived at the Federal Reserve Bank?

A second obstacle to the clearing of the crimes lay in the ignorance by even the victim that a theft occurred. For example, G. H. Walker, the brokerage firm that served as one of the unwitting "suppliers" of Marvins, received a $100,000 Treasury bill on July 8, 1969. The piece was not missed until August 19, 1969. Some brokerage houses and banks that serve as custodians for paper treasures conduct infrequent audits of their presumed inventory. Unless the customer wants to fondle his assets or more likely desires to trade them, there's no reason why the custodian should ascertain that the securities actually are on the premises. As a result, pieces like common stocks that have no maturity date and long-term bonds can be removed from safekeeping and marketed without owner, caretaker, customer, or FBI ever the wiser.

Whether it was a G. H. Walker piece or one from Marine Midland that ignited the investigation into the Treasury bill business in Boston is unknown. Conceivably, the cause of FBI agent Robert Sheehan's vigilance was Vincent Teresa. As Teresa testified, he had been the prime mover in the first venture of $34,000 in Marvins. At the time he already suffered from a terminal case of the feds. He had several heavy indictments over his head. In fact, from his share of the $22,000 brought to him by Cefalo and Chiodi, Teresa gave a bail bondsman $5,000 and his lawyer $2,500. Possibly, Teresa or someone who had an inkling of his activities primed the authorities to study the migratory habits of Treasury bills in the Boston area.

Above everything else, the case of the Marvins proves how swiftly organized crime delivers the goods. The Morgan piece left the Wall Street premises on Thursday afternoon, October 16. In three days it had moved from The Person through several more hands, was sold by the fence, transported to Boston, and finally delivered to Marvin Karger, who was at the Town Bank and Trust early Monday, like any go-getter in business.

Furthermore, the first bill recovered from the Morgan robbery would appear to have offered the freshest clues to The Person as well as to the entire criminal chain that participated. But even with the aid of Teresa, a small-timer to be sure and still a part of the fringe, the investigators could not penetrate the conspiracy. In retrospect, the recovery of the first piece from Morgan was not a true triumph of detection but a fluke. If it were not that Karger's previous transactions had alerted the FBI, the Morgan piece would have been cashed and in all probability Morgan or its insurers liable, since the note was not yet on any hot list.

V

The Plumber's Caper

Nearly one month after FBI agent Sheehan recognized the last Marvin as a parcel out of the Morgan Guaranty lode, a second note came to the attention of the authorities. In this instance the recovery owed nothing to any sharp-eyed Feebee on the watch. In fact the whole affair was a demonstration of nonfeasance by the agents.

On November 18, 1969, *The New York Times* carried a story on page fourteen about an accountant named Robert Rosenberger who walked into the "staid brokerage firm" of Laidlaw & Company across the street from the Morgan Guaranty Trust at 23 Wall Street. He asked the company to cash a $1,000,000 Treasury note, number 226813A. When officers of Laidlaw & Company inquired as to how Rosenberger acquired the note he answered, according to *The Times*, "I received it from a rich kid out on the Island who got it from his parents." The unnamed scion purportedly wished to negotiate the item surreptitiously because his family was in the banking business and it would be embarrassing for word to get out that a $1,000,000 note had been cashed. It was hardly a story that Laidlaw & Company could have been expected to swallow. *The Times* reported that the firm requested a delay until it could confirm the authenticity of the bill. The newspaper said initially Rosenberger, an attorney from New Rochelle named Ernest Milchman, and a Long Island businessman, Lester Spivak, were arrested and then subsequently an associate of Spivak, attorney Harold Goerlich, was also taken into custody.

Not only was the fiction offered Laidlaw & Company incredible, but the tale told by *The Times* was false as well, quite probably because the investigators bungled the case badly. The fiction in *The Times* derived its inspiration from two possible sources: a legitimate desire temporarily to conceal the fonts of government information, and, less acceptably, a coverup for sloppy detective work.

Lester Spivak, 34 years old at the time, started his occupational career by training as a plumber. As new housing continued to boom on Long Island, Spivak established his own business, installing cesspools. When a slowdown hit the housing market, Spivak was caught between his debtors and his creditors. He entered into bankruptcy proceedings and the lawyer recommended to him for the paper work was Harold Goerlich. Out of that relationship came the genesis of something called Swiss Capital Limited. Spivak and Goerlich tied into a loose alliance as money-finders, an artful service to fit the needs of those with highly speculative propositions. Spivak credited Goerlich with the name of the organization, which conjured up a genie of international finance. Spivak's role was to find people who needed capital; Goerlich supposedly located would-be backers.

The former plumber and current money-broker had gone to Rosenberger with the Treasury bill. The proposition from Spivak specified a fee of $25,000 for Rosenberger plus the difference between $800,000 and whatever the $1,000,000 bill brought in the market, perhaps another $140,000 or so. After Spivak left, Rosenberger telephoned Laidlaw—contrary to *The Times,* no one actually traveled to the Wall Street address—and attempted to learn if the bill could be cashed. Informed subsequently that the note was stolen and a stop on it supposedly listed with every banking institution around the world, Rosenberger telephoned the FBI.

On November 13, in the evening, Lester Spivak drove his rented blue Cadillac Eldorado to Manhattan and went to the offices of Rosenberger to deliver the T bill. Waiting for him were FBI agents who immediately put him under arrest. Ernest Milchman, described as an attorney for Rosenberger, also was present.

Under the command of Andy Watson, the men of the FBI questioned Lester Spivak for a number of hours. He dropped the nonsense about an heir who wanted to avoid publicity about the sale of the bill and directly implicated Harold Goerlich. Spivak contended that the note had been handed to him by Goerlich who had vouched for the legitimacy of its ownership. In fact, he said, his associate had accompanied him on the trip to Manhattan to drop off the security with Rosenberger. The plan had been for Goerlich to wait in the Cadillac in a parking lot. When the agents went to the vehicle they found it empty.

Spivak's personal life had become as complicated as his business one. He had a wife and four children but he was actually spending most of his time with another woman, Nancy Dyer. She had become increasingly worried when Spivak failed to return from his visit to Manhattan. She telephoned a number of his haunts but he was of course not to be found. Nancy Dyer did receive a call from Harold Goerlich who instructed that if Lester Spivak telephoned her he should immediately get in touch with his associate. Early the next morning, Nancy Dyer and Harold Goerlich went to the offices of Swiss Capital Limited. While she continued to make telephone calls in search of her lover, she observed Goerlich going through the files in the office and stuffing papers into his attaché case.

From there the pair went to Nancy Dyer's home. She had a relative on the New York City Police Department and as a last resort asked him to locate the missing man. Looking out her window, as she later testified, Nancy Dyer observed Harold Goerlich burning papers in the barbecue pit. Shortly after, Nancy Dyer received word from her relative that Spivak was in the hands of the FBI for attempting to sell a stolen security. Goerlich subsequently was also picked up on a warrant for allegedly participating in the same crime.

When Assistant U.S. Attorney Michael Pollack studied the record it was obvious to him that there were grave weaknesses in the government's case. Lester Spivak, who had admitted his own guilt, was the sole witness against the accountant. The failure rested entirely with the FBI team investigating the incident. Once the Bureau had been alerted by Robert Rosenberger that Lester Spivak possessed a stolen T bill and expected to deliver it to Rosenberger's office, elementary procedure should have called for surveillance of Lester Spivak to identify his associates, and perhaps to discover from whom he obtained the item. At the very least, an agent could have testified whether anyone had traveled to Manhattan with Spivak.

A second stroke of ineptitude lay in the failure to immediately get a search warrant and go through Lester Spivak's office to find any papers that would serve either to support Spivak's assertion that he was a blameless dupe or reveal who else might be involved. An FBI expert who ex-

amined the ashes determined that some papers had indeed
been torched in the barbecue pit at Nancy Dyer's place.
But he could not tell the nature of these documents.

Michael Pollack, reviewing the record, says, "The FBI
made the mistake of thinking that Spivak's confession was
all that they needed."

The errors of the FBI were even less understandable
since both Spivak and Goerlich were already under investigation in connection with another matter that centered
on stolen securities. Lester Spivak had tried to negotiate
thousands of dollars of stocks owned by one Gerald Matson with Bi Planning Co., a Long Island over-the-counter
stock brokerage house. The government had charged that
Matson's signature had been forged, that Goerlich had endorsed the signatures as authentic, and that Spivak was the
conspirator assigned the task of disposing of the pieces. Bi
Planning had been told that Gerald Matson had put up the
stocks as collateral on a loan, defaulted on his payments
and the securities were to be redeemed to cover the
moneys due.

Although the attempt to sell off the Gerald Matson
stocks to Bi Planning occurred in the middle of October, a
month before the T-bill incident, Goerlich stood in the
dock first as the defendant in regard to the Morgan Guaranty Trust's note. Robert Rosenberger and Ernest Milchman both narrated their tales of the visit from Spivak and
the call to Laidlaw & Company. Curiously, when Edward
Wuensche, a convicted trafficker in stolen securities, testified before the Permanent Subcommittee on Investigations of the Senate Committee on Government Operations,
which was looking into such transactions in 1971, he said
of Milchman, "I met him in 1967 and 1968 in New York
City. He is a close associate of Emanuel Lester. Milchman
is knowledgeable in the overseas aspects of stolen securities. He has been arrested for possession of stolen securi-

ties." How it was that the holders of the Treasury bill selected Rosenberger to negotiate the piece was never revealed. However, for notifying the FBI, once he was alerted by Laidlaw & Company that the note was stolen, Rosenberger qualified for a reward from Morgan Guaranty Trust. Until the maturity dates were reached, the price for recovery was five points.

Lester Spivak recounted to the jury how he had been given the $1,000,000 Treasury bill by Harold Goerlich. He said he received a written statement from one Thomas Miley: "Please be advised that I am in receipt of one Treasury bill, number 226813A," and it vouched for the authenticity of the item. Thomas Miley was apparently a figment of the conspiracy. Spivak contended that he had no idea there was anything irregular about the operation and that Harold Goerlich had accompanied him as far as a parking lot near Rosenberger's office. While an attendant in the parking lot recalled two men having been in the blue Eldorado, he could not identify either one as Goerlich, or for that matter Spivak. Spivak's estranged wife told the court that she received a telephone call from Harold Goerlich on the night that her husband temporarily vanished in which Goerlich purportedly said, "If you hear from Lester, tell him it's better for him to take the rap by himself." Nancy Dyer also testified about the events that took place in the offices of Swiss Capital Limited and at her home. There was, however, no evidence at all that directly tied Harold Goerlich to the attempt to pass the bill. Actually, under New York State law, Goerlich could not even have been brought to trial since evidence based upon the word of an accomplice (Spivak) must be corroborated. Federal law, however, does permit prosecution solely on the word of an accomplice to a crime.

The attorney for the defense went to work on Lester Spivak's credibility. From the chief prosecution witness,

Goerlich's counsel drew admission that he had lied to potential clients by describing himself as a vice president of Swiss Capital. He had taken retainers from clients without obtaining loans for them. There was an insinuation that Spivak could not or did not try to raise the capital for these customers. He was shown to have written rubber checks, violated the Workman's Compensation Act, traveled to Europe with Nancy Dyer while leaving his wife and four children home, even to the extent that they were currently on welfare.

The government was unable to proffer additional evidence of Goerlich's participation. He appeared in his own defense, swearing he had no idea what Spivak was engaged in and that he had not driven to New York City with his associate on the evening in question.

The jury found the defendant not guilty. In the subsequent trial for the theft of the securities from Gerald Matson, a second individual, Lazzaro A. San Giovanni, joined Harold Goerlich in the dock. San Giovanni was also accused by Spivak of having been a partner with Goerlich to negotiate the stolen securities. Defense counsel again shattered Spivak's believability with a listing of his sins, to which had also been added now the conviction of "conspiracy to possess, conceal, sell and dispose" of the $1,000,000 Treasury bill. The verdicts returned for Goerlich and San Giovanni were not guilty.

Lester Spivak for his cooperation with the government's case served no time in prison. He received a divorce from his wife, married Nancy Dyer, and with the help of the Justice Department created a new identity for himself in another part of the United States. The last report that Michael Pollack had of Lester Spivak was that he had achieved a modest success in his new and honest role.

VI

The Luxembourg Caper

The first two incompleted passes of the Treasury bills employed some individuals with some knowledge that they dealt with stolen securities. The third try introduced another kind of participant, the businessman mesmerized into eccentric behavior by the promise of a generous commission in what bore the trappings of a legitimate deal. Another new aspect was a change of venue from the U.S. to foreign territory.

Salvatore Cuomo, a 40-year-old resident of New Haven, Connecticut, trailed no criminal record in 1969. His visible means of support, however, seemed vague. He hung around a meat-packing plant, occasionally talked in an abstract fashion about buying into the place. Supposedly, he sold real estate out of his home but nobody ever discovered who his customers were. He had two years of high school, served honorably in the army for a couple of years, was the father of three daughters, and made a genial but staid appearance.

On the other hand, Frederick Nelson, a balding, husky six-footer, was a 43-year-old New Yorker with a substantive vocation. A certified public accountant since 1950, Nelson had been educated at City College in New York. His clients were an unexceptional run of businesses and institutions that provided him with a comfortable living. Separated from his wife, Nelson limited his vices to the local cultural scene and vacations at the finer foreign resorts.

Salvatore Cuomo and Frederick Nelson first met in the spring of 1969. Nelson occasionally served as a geiger counter for prospective investors. And Salvatore Cuomo claimed to earn some of his livelihood by locating the Nelsons of the world for clients in need of capital. A third party aware of their round hole, round peg natures introduced them. The first piece of joint business concerned efforts to arrange a $6,000,000 loan for Emery Pictures, a company that claimed it would use the funds to obtain the licenses for the entire film library of Republic Pictures. The product was basically a mix of B features, a handful of chintzy spectaculars starring a female friend of the one-time head of Republic, and the real wealth, dozens of Roy Rogers and Gene Autry westerns that could fill thousands of hours of Saturday morning kid time on TV. The collateral for the loan was to be the licenses that belonged to Emery.

"Before I even became involved," said Nelson, "I checked Cuomo out with Dun and Bradstreet and Bishop's." The reports indicated no transgressions by the New Haven broker; on the other hand they did not reveal any positive information either. There was a third man present at some of the sessions Nelson had with Cuomo. He was Ignazio (Benny) Marchese, a resident of Bridgeport, Connecticut, and Nelson considered him sort of a traveling companion and part-time chauffeur for Cuomo.

"He rarely spoke, never entered into the business conversation," said Nelson. "He seemed like a kindly, genial grandfather." Nelson did not look into Benny Marchese's background; had he done so he might have been surprised at exploits attributed to the grandfather.

"We came very close on the TV deal," said Nelson. "At one point an investor offered $5.5 million but the people at Emery felt it wasn't quite good enough. The whole thing collapsed, after I spent many many hours in conferences with lawyers, investors, and Emery executives. It was a dead loss for me."

Cuomo, who had actually done very little of the negotiating once he contacted Nelson, now approached the accountant with a variety of small proposals such as a nursing home. But these were even more ephemeral than the TV proposition. "I told Cuomo I had no need for this kind of speculation. I would not participate in any more contingent deals," said Nelson.

Salvatore Cuomo then broached an entirely new kind of proposition. He asked if Nelson knew of any place in the world where the anonymity of an owner could be protected if the individual wished to negotiate a Treasury bill or use the T bill as collateral. Frederick Nelson did not ordinarily deal in T bills but on the subject of foreign banking he had some expertise. He had connections in banks in Beirut, Zurich, and the tiny principality of Luxembourg. He had serviced European clients that included the Hungarian flag airline and an agency of the French government that tried to keep track of U.S. advances to filmmakers and couturiers in France, for the purpose of assessing taxes.

Based upon all of this experience, Nelson cited perhaps half a dozen locations where confidentiality could be expected. Cuomo remarked that he was speaking of securities worth between two and three million dollars. Nelson quickly added one caveat for any sale of Treasury bills. "They must be verified, the bills cannot be lost or counterfeits."

Curiously, Cuomo in his next encounter with the accountant switched the discussion to the subject of buried treasure. He asked Nelson whether he would be interested in the salvage of some very old U.S. currency, paper money that had been buried in the ground during the 1930s and had only recently been exhumed. According to Cuomo, the money had begun to decompose during its long stay in the earth and he described the bills as "fused together." Cuomo explained that the recently discovered hoard of $2,100,000 belonged to an old man in Florida. Like the Treasury bill proposal, the principal required secrecy for the redemption of the valuables. The old man, asserted Cuomo, wished to keep his wealth secret from his avaricious sons and daughters-in-law.

Frederick Nelson was friendly with two former government officials, Joseph Abraham and Michael Artis. Both of them had international business experience. Abraham was currently an executive with a large oil company and Artis had until recently been with the Justice Department.

Artis, as an attorney with friends in the Justice Department, undertook to learn the ramifications of redemption of long buried currency through foreign banks. After several consultations the three men agreed that there seemed to be nothing unlawful about the stipulation of anonymity. "Artis," said Nelson, "also asked around to make certain that the Justice Department was not looking for any large sums of money that had been buried or disappeared during the 1930s." Again the answers were favorable to the enterprise.

In the early summer of 1969, Salvatore Cuomo met with Nelson and Abraham and handed over a packet of somewhat deteriorated paper money. "It wasn't fragile or crumbly to the touch," said Nelson. "It was more like a seven-layer cake of money in which you couldn't separate one bill from another." Serial numbers were fed to Artis who again sought to discover if law enforcement agencies were hunting these bills. Everything still came up legitimate.

The plan was for Abraham to fly to Switzerland, at his own expense. There he would locate a bank that would perform the delicate job of resurrecting the currency. "The Swiss were supposed to have experience and skills for re-storing postage stamps and currency," said Nelson. "We rejected the possibility of hiring an individual with this ca-pacity because we also wanted to use an organization that would have enough experience to determine whether the money was genuine. The last thing we wanted was to wind up with a couple of million in counterfeit."

If Abraham found the right bank and the operation on the fused currency was successful, Cuomo was to immedi-ately fly to Geneva with the balance of the rotten money. Cuomo was to pay off the owner of the bills from his 50 percent share of the proceeds. Nelson and company were to split the remainder. Expenses for the travelers and the Swiss bank's fee would come off the top.

In Geneva, Abraham swiftly discovered a bank whose technicians restored the sample of money, which amounted to $200. It was exacting work by skilled workers and for their efforts the Swiss asked 10 percent of the cur-rency, or $210,000 of the $2,100,000. That was agreeable to all parties. But a snag suddenly developed. Cuomo re-ported that the old man now refused to yield the rest of the treasure. Abraham waited around Geneva for a week, at his own expense. Irate at the collapse of the scheme after he had invested time and about $1,000 on the project, he flew back to New York in midsummer.

In the months that followed Salvatore Cuomo offered apologies for the stubbornness of his client. To atone for the imposition he offered at the end of October another project. He had another client who owned a $1,000,000 Treasury bill. The possessor was willing to sacrifice one-half of anything beyond $500,000 if the bill could be negotiated under the right circumstances. These consisted only of a guarantee of his anonymity. The proposition meant a pot of well over $200,000 for Cuomo, Nelson, and the others to share. "That sounds like an excessive commission, perhaps," said Nelson. "But it was really based upon the previous scheme to redeem the cakes of old bills. It was Cuomo's way of making amends to us." Actually, the fee for the Treasury bill negotiation works out to considerably less than the buried money deal even on a percentage basis. But what is most peculiar is the size of the commission for what are the ordinary services of a broker. Normally, the fee for handling a T bill through either a stockbroker or a bank would be figured at roughly one percent. On a $1,000,000 note that approximates somewhere around $9,000. (Remember, T bills are always sold at discounts; face value is not collected until maturity.) Neither banks nor brokerage houses that must do a certain amount of paper work to arrange the transaction feel themselves exploited on the basis of a one percent commission. But Cuomo was contracting for a commission that amounted to better than 20 percent.

Assuming that the T bill was not stolen and not a counterfeit, only two explanations for the desire for anonymity would appear to exist. Either the client wished to keep secret from the Internal Revenue Service a large asset or he hoped to hide the interest collected. Since the latter amounted to perhaps 5 percent of the face value, the desire to go through a Swiss bank seems pointless. And in truth, as Frederick Nelson knew from his experience in foreign banking circles, the reputation for secrecy in Swiss banks is based upon some misconceptions. The Swiss protect clients from the beady eyes of U.S. tax collectors and other snoops if the depositors do a significant amount of their banking in the country. However, the Swiss have no compunctions about one-shotters who consider the country's banks laundromats for funds. Unofficially, the Swiss do reveal casual transactions to U.S. agencies. Cuomo's million-dollar note would fall under that heading. For Frederick Nelson and his associates, however, there was no risk in their participation so long as the note was not stolen. It was Cuomo's client who allegedly sought to cover up an asset or income.

Early in November of 1969, Salvatore Cuomo brought to Frederick Nelson's office a photocopy of the Treasury bill. Nelson prudently visited the offices of the National Bank of North America where he did business. "I knew two officers of the bank," said Nelson, "and I asked if they had lists of stolen Treasury bills. They had a list for items missing from Bache and Co. and from Goodbody. But they had no list for Morgan Guaranty. I wasn't satisfied and I went to a third officer. He didn't have a Morgan list either but I kept pushing them until finally he telephoned the main office. I sat at his desk while he read the number of the bill over the telephone. The voice at the other end of the phone said, 'It's not on our list.' "

The bank executive suggested to Nelson that if he wanted absolute confirmation of the authenticity of the bill and its ownership he could call the U.S. Treasury. "I considered doing that," said Nelson. "But I decided that would be an unwarranted betrayal of trust since Cuomo and his client had come to me with the expectation of confidentiality. In effect, I would be turning them in."

Since Nelson's previous experience in foreign banks had not included the negotiation of a Treasury bill he consulted with a New York firm of lawyers with offices that engaged in the practice of law abroad. "They suggested that on my arrival in Switzerland I call one of their partners who was friendly with the officials of the Luxembourg bank. Again the Treasury bill would be verified as having not been stolen. Furthermore, I was advised that it would be preferable to have a non-American actually cash the bill. In that fashion, the likelihood of advice to the U.S. about the redemption of the bill would be lessened."

While the preliminaries to negotiation of the Treasury note went on, Abraham and Artis continued to fume over Cuomo's inept plot to exchange the decayed money. There was a meeting at Nelson's home, out of which he also conducted his business, and all four men were present. Abraham, still exasperated over his $1,000 wasted on the abortive trip to Geneva, demanded of Cuomo whether the buried money was real or limited to $200 and an active imagination.

Cuomo replied, "Help Frederick with the Treasury note." He promised to continue to nag the owner of the underground wealth. To sweeten the atmosphere, Cuomo intimated that his share of the T bill proceeds would be just enough front money for him to make an outright buy of the $2,100,000 in decomposed bills.

Once more, Nelson called upon Artis for legal aid. He sifted through the banking laws and concluded that so long as the bill was not stolen, there was nothing illegal about the operation.

At the end of the meeting, Abraham and Artis vaguely agreed to be parties to the deal although their roles were minimal. Artis had supplied some legal advice. Abraham telephoned a friend in Italy with Swiss bank connections. He was out to recoup his losses in the previous venture. He also volunteered to find a non-American to present the T bill. The pair lived in Washington, D.C., and as they headed for home, misgivings about the entire affair nagged at them. By the time they had landed in Washington, both decided they wanted no part of the T-bill deal. From a telephone booth they called New York to inform Frederick Nelson of their determination. They discovered that Nelson had already taken off for Switzerland. To ensure their position, Artis and Abraham cabled Nelson declaring themselves out.

When Nelson arrived in Zurich on November 21 he immediately contacted the local offices of the law firm that he had consulted in the U.S. One of the partners took the number of the Treasury bill and said he would check it with the bank in Luxembourg. Two or three days later, Nelson received word from the lawyer that the bank said the T bill was not on any hot list and therefore could be negotiated.

Before leaving the United States, Frederick Nelson had made several interesting arrangements. He had not actually carried the Treasury bill on his person but instead mailed it from New York to what the Swiss call a Fiduciaire, a licensed firm empowered to serve as a kind of proxy between a client and the banks. A Fiduciaire can make deposits and withdrawals for its customer without ever revealing anything about identity except the critical question of Swiss or foreign citizenship. Foreigners pay a higher tax than the local people.

From the Fiduciaire, Nelson retrieved the Treasury bill still sealed in an envelope. "I mailed it because I didn't want to risk losing it," explained Nelson. By mailing it, Nelson removed the possibility that he might be found in possession of the paper inside the United States' jurisdiction.

Through the offices of Abraham, an individual who was a "non-American" had been recruited to visit the bank with the security. It was to be a woman coming from Beirut and her name, given by someone with a flair for romance, was to be Madame L'Orient. The first disruption in plans was word that Madame L'Orient would not be able to come to Zurich because of some domestic problem.

"It had to be a woman," said Nelson, "because the Luxembourg bank had been told a woman with the name Madame L'Orient would bring the Treasury bill." Nelson neatly disposed of the difficulty by hiring the administrative assistant to the Swiss Fiduciaire, a Mrs. Monique Dubois.

Nelson's representative crossed the border to Luxembourg on November 25. At the bank in Luxembourg, Mrs. Dubois, who had announced herself as Madame L'Orient, was quickly told that the Treasury bill which she presented was stolen and definitely not negotiable. Bank officers returned the piece to her and she carried the tidings to Frederick Nelson. "I was furious," he remembered. "I called the law offices and, expressing my indignation, asked how the hell the bank could have said the bill was negotiable yesterday but not today. I was really unable to understand anything about what happened because after all I had even checked the bill in the United States."

Since the Treasury bill had been handed back to Mrs. Dubois and neither she nor Nelson had been detained or questioned by authorities, he reasoned that he faced no difficulties, either in Switzerland or in the United States. "I did wrestle with what I felt was an ethical problem," said Nelson. "I wondered about revealing Cuomo's name to police in the United States. Otherwise I felt no loyalty to him. In any event, I assumed that while the Luxembourg bank had refused to accept the bill, they would not report the matter to the police. And if they did advise the police, when they came to see me I would cooperate completely. But I did not intend to turn in the bill voluntarily. That was a big mistake on my part."

Nelson hung around Switzerland for several more days

before reserving a seat on a flight back to New York. At the Swiss airport, as he checked through passport control, two gentlemen in plainclothes asked him to follow them to an office. His baggage was searched, the note found. From there he was driven to a Swiss prison.

The Luxembourg bankers had actually reported to both Swiss and U.S. officials that the stolen million-dollar note had been offered by Mrs. Dubois. When interrogated she of course identified the principal as Frederick Nelson, a U.S. citizen. During the three days following the attempt to negotiate the piece, the Justice Department in the U.S. had gone through the process of securing a warrant for Nelson's arrest and forwarding it to the embassy in Switzerland. But first, the Swiss were determined to see if Nelson had violated any of their laws.

"Under Swiss law," said Nelson, an unfortunate expert by personal experience, "you can be detained for as long as a year without any charges pressed against you. A Swiss citizen has some rights similar to habeas corpus but as a foreigner you have nothing. I spent a month in the slammer trying to explain what had happened and trying to protect Mrs. Dubois and show that she was not really involved.

"It was all very difficult. The Swiss lawyer assigned to assist me did not speak English or French, which I did. The prosecutor pretended not to speak or understand English but he really did. It was only after five days of this that someone from the embassy visited me. As a result my family and friends were able to learn where I was."

One of those who remained ignorant was Salvatore Cuomo who called Nelson's home several times and asked the housekeeper, "When is he coming back, when do I get my money?"

Nelson found the Swiss jailers very trying. "Everything was so impersonal; you were dehumanized" (not truly different from the U.S.). The establishment was short on the amenities. "You were allowed to shower only once a week and I never was able to get any of my clothes cleaned during the month I spent in the prison. On the other hand, I could get telephone calls from the outside with no difficulty and my lawyer could visit me at any time."

After two weeks, the Swiss prosecutor told the American that he had been arrested on the strength of the warrant from the United States. The Swiss, satisfied that he actually committed no crime against their banking laws, were now prepared to honor the warrant. However, Nelson would be obliged to spend four to six weeks in his present abode until the matter of extradition was settled. "I told him I would waive extradition," said Nelson. "I wanted nothing more than to return to the States as quickly as possible. It still took another two weeks for them to process my papers. I was taken to the airport. A representative of the embassy waited to be certain that I made the plane."

When he arrived at New York's Kennedy Airport, Nelson remained in his seat while the other passengers disembarked. He sensed that there would be a reception committee and he was correct. Agents of the FBI boarded the airplane and escorted him off. Although he was under arrest, Nelson does not recall that anyone read him his rights. Nevertheless, his baggage was thoroughly inspected and he was subjected to a strip search. He made no statement to the agents, insisting that he wished to consult with his attorney first. After fingerprinting, he was released on $10,000 bond.

Meanwhile, the Bureau ran a fingerprint check on the T bill. Their expert reported that he did not find any prints on the bill matching those of Marvin Karger. The wild hope that everything might unravel as a plot between Bostonians and the crew involved in the Luxembourg caper was quashed.

There was never any real question in the mind of Nelson and his lawyer that he could eventually cooperate fully with the investigation. Accompanied by counsel, the accountant subsequently made a complete statement about events to the investigators. Nelson received a bad scare when the high echelon employees of the National Bank of North America had no recollection of any attempt to check out the T bill. Fortunately for Nelson, some of the lesser clerks at the bank did remember the accountant's perseverance as he scurried from office to office asking for authentication.

During his time of questioning, Nelson received a telephone call from Salvatore Cuomo. Nelson answered very guardedly and invited his erstwhile partner to meet with Nelson's lawyer "to discuss the matter." The New Haven man did not attempt to arrange a conference, however.

Then there was a telephone call from the hitherto silent observer. "This is Benny," said the voice, which Nelson recognized as belonging to Marchese. He asked why Nelson had failed to turn over his share of the proceeds from the T-bill sale.

"I can't discuss it now," replied the cautious Nelson. Marchese insisted that Nelson "call Sal." Instead, Nelson hung up and reported the conversation to his acquaintances at the FBI. In early February of 1970, Marchese suddenly accosted Nelson in front of the latter's home. The elderly man mumbled that his life was in danger and that he was being dunned by unidentified individuals for $250,000. "He wanted me to give back the money," Nelson testified later when the whole matter finally went to trial.

"I told him that he's crazy. Hadn't he heard I had been

arrested and that the note was a stolen one." Actually, it was highly possible, even probable, that Cuomo and Marchese knew nothing of what had happened. Although Nelson was seized by the Swiss in late November, there was no public announcement in the U.S. press until March 4, 1970. The net result of Marchese's importunate plea to Nelson was to implicate himself firmly in the scheme to cash the T bill. As soon as the elderly Bridgeport man left Nelson, the accountant telephoned his FBI interrogators about the incident.

The government did not immediately arrest Cuomo and Marchese. Several weeks passed before Nelson, through his attorney, was satisfied that his cooperation would be fully recognized by the government and no charges brought against him. The feds delayed in hopes that Cuomo and Marchese, thinking Nelson had not revealed their names, might be indiscreet enough to contact the original source of the T bill. Neither man obliged, however. Once arraigned, they insisted on their innocence.

Nelson was not indicted or named as an unindicted co-conspirator. Artis and Abraham were charged by the grand jury as unindicted co-conspirators and Salvatore Cuomo and Benny Marchese became the defendants.

Largely on the basis of the testimony offered by Nelson, Artis, and Abraham, the jury found Cuomo and Marchese guilty. Neither of them took the stand in his own defense. Judge Constance Baker Motley studied the probation reports on Cuomo. His physician described him as "friendly, generous, a kind neighbor." His brother, a retired air force lieutenant colonel, praised his concern and attention to the military man's family while the officer served overseas. A psychiatrist labeled him "gullible, with no symptoms of psychosis or severe neurosis." Judge Motley hit him with eight years.

Ignazio Marchese, almost an invisible man while the

plot hatched, continued to be a cipher when the probation reports on him were filed with Judge Motley. There was no one to speak favorably of him; he had served seven years for a federal narcotics rap and another stretch for armed robbery. Judge Motley sentenced him to ten years.

Frederick Nelson bore no rancor toward the two who had brought him close to disaster. He was not in court during the testimony of other witnesses nor did he know anything of Marchese's previous record until five years after the trial. He still could not believe that the kindly, grandfatherly Benny Marchese deserved what amounted to a near life sentence for a 68-year-old. However, Judge Motley was undoubtedly influenced by suggestions that Marchese was far less innocent than his looks; he was credited with having connections into organized crime.

Michael Artis suffered some sharp reverses in his career as a direct consequence of his involvement. He had been proposed for a high government post and the nomination vanished once he was identified as a co-conspirator, although unindicted. Abraham went back to the oil business. Frederick Nelson picked up his life as an accountant. Occasionally, his connection with the crime surfaces during a discussion with clients and the matter has cost him some business as well as embarrassment. He was also notified by the Swiss government that because of his role in the plot he was barred from Swiss soil for ten years. "I brought this up with the U.S. Attorney," said Nelson, "and he agreed that since I had been innocent this was unfair. He wrote a letter to that effect to the Swiss authorities. They replied that in view of the circumstances they would reduce the period to five years."

If one accepts the innocence of Frederick Nelson, his entanglement has a kind of somnambulistic quality. He is the legitimate professional led step by step, prospect by prospect, into what eventually turns out to be a nightmare of improbity. It is only with hindsight that the final scene bulks so obviously as felonious.

Like any good accountant, Nelson wrote the whole thing off as a bad investment, a loss to be filed and forgotten, if possible. He has stuffed away memories of the incident in a locked drawer of the mind. He never compared notes with his friends Artis or Abraham. Nor did he inquire of the FBI for added details. Still, he admits that for all of his common-sense dismissal of the matter as a kind of accident, he finds the entire business emotionally distressing whenever it arises.

VII
The Porn Merchants

Behind the Luxembourg caper were the erroneous beliefs that foreigners are more gullible or less scrupulous than the folks back home. Those supposed to be particularly susceptible to the fictions were international traders in other underworld goods, such as dealers in dope and pornography who had prospered abroad. It was inevitable that some of these merchants would add hot Morgan paper to their lines.

On February 7, 1970, in Munich, West Germany, a Canadian national, Bernard Reindolph, a.k.a. Bernard Randolph, was placed under arrest by the German police and accused of an attempt to sell a $100,000 Treasury bill, identified as a piece of the Morgan Guaranty loot.

Reindolph, a 41-year-old native of Montreal, married and the father of six kids, was not unknown to the Royal Canadian Mounted Police. But his trade, until he was picked up in Europe, had been the marketing of pornographic materials.

With Reindolph at the time of arrest was one of his associates in the porn game, Georges Merceau, another Canadian. The interrogation of Reindolph, led mainly by a representative of the Swedish police, initially drew from him an "I was framed" routine. While he demanded to consult an attorney before he would talk about the Treasury bill matter, Reindolph supplied some sketchy information on his actions.

"In May, 1969, I came to London. Before that I was in the pornographic business under a variety of names. I ran the business alone. In London I tried to set up a pin-up sales operation, but I had no luck. I met with Daniel Howard who ran an art gallery. We have been in business together in Copenhagen and Stockholm."

Reindolph rambled on, dropping further names in his pornographic associations. An American ran a pornographic business in Copenhagen and he was a partner with Merceau. Reindolph became a kind of traveling representative of the firm, doing much of his buying in Copenhagen. "Merceau financed me," confessed Reindolph. Various American visitors and residents obligingly mailed bundles of porno materials to the States for a time, but U.S. Customs became extremely suspicious of any packages from what was considered the porn capital of the world.

Reindolph moved his base to Stockholm because he found he could distribute his "literature" more easily from there. One of his dealers, a Swede named Roald Axelsson, introduced Reindolph to a 57-year-old businessman named Berl Gutenberg whose vague interests included horses and real estate as well as the porn business. Gutenberg bragged that a diplomat, using his immunity, assisted him in the export of smut. Reindolph proposed that the Swedish entrepreneur put up the money for a Stockholm nightclub but Gutenberg showed no interest. Meanwhile,

Reindolph traveled through Europe, toting suitcases of porn to Vienna, Munich, Torremolinos, and the like.

On one of these trips in early February, said Reindolph, he dropped considerable cash in a Wiesbaden casino while in the company of his associate Georges Merceau. On the fourth of the month, Merceau supposedly handed him a sealed envelope to be mailed to Intercontinental Franchize, Attn: T. Berger. Reindolph was asked to hang on to the letter for safekeeping. In their rooms at the Carlton Hotel in Munich, Merceau asked Reindolph to open the envelope. "Inside there was some kind of paper," Reindolph told his inquisitors in Munich. "Then two men came into the room, examined the paper and we were all arrested." Merceau, however, had told the cops another story, insisting he knew nothing of "the paper" in question. Reindolph scoffed, "It is my opinion that Merceau is covering for somebody." He added, "Merceau is a real crook. He is also a swindler."

It was a tale that the listeners found hard to believe, particularly since they had already compiled a dossier on Reindolph and some of his colleagues that implicated Reindolph but not Merceau.

Two days after the Munich arrest, Reindolph abandoned his bluff and laid his dismal cards face up on the table for the benefit of the investigators. Toward the end of December, 1969, Reindolph said he had returned to Montreal for a visit. While in Canada he renewed his acquaintance with a man named Robert Hite, a Canadian who at one time owned a laundry but had other things in mind than cleaning clothes.

Hite and another Canadian, Thomas Berger, had a proposition for the foreign trader, the sale of Treasury bills abroad. Reindolph protested, "My line is pornography." Hite persisted, "We handle street [stocks] stuff and we can get it by the carload." He spoke of up to $15,000,000 worth of securities on hand. He also said he had for sale one hundred pounds of pure uranium, which would require lead-lined containers to ship, and $500,000 in West German securities.

Reindolph had not prospered in the pornography business and he was willing to try anything to end his financial drought. The new venture got off on a slightly disagreeable note, however. Hite, after securing Reindolph's agreement to participate, advised his confederate not to strike out for himself. "Don't play any games," said the laundry proprietor, who referred to "the old man in Buffalo."

Hite, said Reindolph, talked of connections with "a family in Chicago," but he was not a member because he came from "the wrong ethnic background." Hite in fact was more like a client of the family. He admitted he owed "them" gambling debts of more than $275,000.

Bernard Reindolph then flew back to Stockholm where he conferred with Roald Axelsson and Berl Gutenberg about the possibilities of selling securities that were not on hot lists. The two Swedes were most agreeable to the proposition. Reindolph contacted Robert Hite who immediately flew to Stockholm where he was met at the airport by Reindolph and Axelsson. The trio drove to Berl Gutenberg's home. Reindolph inquired of his Canadian partner, "Do you have the stuff?"

Hite answered by producing two $100,000 Treasury bills. Gutenberg was somewhat surprised; he had thought in terms of common stocks. "I can move a carload of this and that," said the Swedish businessman. "But what is the Treasury bill business?"

Robert Hite educated the foreigner. "This here is better than cash in the United States. The government must pay these on demand. It makes no difference if they are stolen or not, the government must pay." Hite left out of his explanation one critical fact. While the government must pay, unless the T bills have been voided, the obligation is limited to a holder in due course, a legitimate owner of such a bill. In any event, the U.S. Treasury does not redeem the securities until maturity. In the interim, banks and brokerage houses trade cash for the bills.

Gutenberg was not reassured. He flatly asked, "Are they counterfeit, are they stolen?"

"No," straightforwardly lied Hite. For his role, Reindolph was promised between 7 and 10 percent. Hite wanted 70 percent, $140,000 net for himself and those he represented. The remaining $40,000 or so was to be divided between Gutenberg and Axelsson. It was a Friday afternoon and the public banking hours had ended. However, Gutenberg telephoned a local bank and arranged to have Axelsson deliver the Treasury bills. He was issued a receipt and told the money for the bills would not be available before Monday.

After Axelsson returned with the receipt and the information, the meeting adjourned. As the three men left Gutenberg's residence, Hite asked, "Is the bank going to check the numbers?"

Axelsson answered, "Probably."

Hite turned to Reindolph. "Didn't you tell him about these?"

"No, we thought street stuff was what you were carrying."

"You better tell him not to check the numbers. The bills might be on the list." Hite seemed to have forgotten entirely that he had said the bills were not stolen only minutes earlier. He also apparently believed that Gutenberg worked through a cooperative bank official. Now it was Reindolph who became agitated with the breach of faith by his fellow Canadian and he denounced him for having lied to Gutenberg.

"If Gutenberg is friendly with the bank director, he can get the bills back or make sure they are not attributed to him in case somebody does check out the numbers," suggested Hite. Reindolph became even angrier at the equivocations of Hite. But neither man advised Gutenberg of the dangers.

It was Gutenberg's belief that his bank would have the money by 2 P.M. on Monday. However, Reindolph figured that if some attempt were to be made to authenticate the Treasury bills that would only be 8 A.M. in New York, well before any of the American financial institutions could respond to communications from Sweden. He was not surprised when Gutenberg informed him that the bank said it would require another day.

Hite seemed unperturbed by events. He wanted a companion to amuse him while he waited. Axelsson, using the artful classified ads of newspapers, located an agreeable woman. The visitors diverted themselves with a trip to the Kaknas Tower with its splendid view, tavern-hopping, sipping beverages at the Sandelius Konditori, a local tearoom. But even Hite eventually became annoyed as the delay of another day dragged on.

Finally, on Tuesday, Berl Gutenberg and Roald Axelsson drove to the Skandinaviska Banken to collect on the Treasury bills. Axelsson waited in the car for the senior member of the enterprise. Gutenberg entered the bank alone. He received a disagreeable reception. He was informed that the securities were stolen ones and there was some talk among the police officials at the scene about placing him under arrest immediately. Gutenberg, however, was able to leave the bank after promising that he would appear at headquarters that afternoon at 2:30.

Axelsson drove the fuming Gutenberg to the Continental Hotel, where the other parties to the transaction waited. Axelsson entered the lobby of the Continental, advised Reindolph and Hite of the unfortunate turn of events. Hite refused even to leave the lobby of the hotel to speak with his erstwhile associate. "He might have been followed," worried Hite. Reindolph, however, accompanied Axelsson back to the automobile where Gutenberg poured out his anger and called Hite "an idiot," and went home to prepare for his session with the police. That evening, Axelsson and Reindolph chauffeured Hite to the airport and he left on a plane without informing his associates of his destination.

Gutenberg actually had not been totally unaware that there might be some difficulties with the T bills. Axelsson, who was present when Reindolph and Hite fell to arguing about the deception practiced by the latter upon Gutenberg, advised the older man of the discussion. Axelsson even suggested that Gutenberg try to retrieve the bills before they could be checked. Gutenberg felt that it was too late for such a maneuver. However, he plotted with Axelsson to protect themselves in the event of any trouble.

Gutenberg drafted a kind of bill of sale in which it was stated that one Verlin G. Stevenson had turned over the Treasury bills to Berl Gutenberg as payment for some real estate property. The paper was typed by Axelsson, witnessed by him, and he supplied the signature for Verlin G. Stevenson. Armed with this document, Gutenberg kept his appointment with the local police. Asked where he made contact with Verlin G. Stevenson, Gutenberg said it was on a visit to Panama.

Meanwhile, the other conspirators had at least temporarily left town. Axelsson accompanied Reindolph on a trip to Germany to assist the Canadian in the distribution of pornographic merchandise under the auspices of Georges Merceau. The itinerary carried them to Vienna where they collected some materials purchased by Merceau. The agents repackaged the stuff and shipped it off to U.S. customers.

In Vienna, as had been pre-planned with Gutenberg, Axelsson and Reindolph collaborated on an effort to breathe more life into Verlin G. Stevenson. Reindolph wrote a short chatty letter to Gutenberg, and Axelsson supplied a signature to match the one employed in the bill of sale. The traveling porn merchants doubled back to Munich and Mainz for more of their business and by telephone arranged for a pair of fun-loving women to meet them on their return to Sweden.

On the last day of January, Reindolph telephoned Axelsson to join him for another visit to Germany, the purpose of which was to ship lewd literature to the U.S. To Axelsson's distress, they met up with Robert Hite in Mainz. The Swede's fears mounted as he observed Hite plunge at the games in Wiesbaden. He watched nervously as Reindolph and Hite conferred by themselves, whispering to one another, turning up the volume of the television set to keep their communications secret even from Axelsson.

Reindolph left for Munich by himself on February 4 to meet with Merceau, leaving Hite and Axelsson behind. When Reindolph failed to telephone from Munich as expected, Hite sent Axelsson in a car to see if he could find him. Halfway between Mainz and Munich on the long journey Axelsson became discouraged enough to turn back. He drove to the Frankfurt airport where he knew Hite was planning to catch a plane. He saw him in the company of an individual that Axelsson subsequently identified from a photograph as the mysterious Thomas Berger, whose name had been on the envelope in the possession of Reindolph the day he was arrested in Munich. After a conference, Axelsson contacted a Swedish private detective to discreetly find out the whereabouts of Reindolph. The private eye brought the glum news that Reindolph was in the hands of the West German police.

Hite and Axelsson managed to reach Georges Merceau who proved a man of very few words on the phone. "I can't talk from here," said Merceau. "Something terrible happened and Reindolph and I have been some place, and you can guess where."

Axelsson and Hite parted company at the airport. The Canadian provided some last-minute counsel. "I've got some influential friends who will protect Reindolph. If you know your own interest, you will forget we ever met." Two or three days later Axelsson, back in Sweden, heard from Hite in Canada. It does not look too good for Reindolph, was the substance of the message.

The bill of sale signed by Verlin G. Stevenson set off a brief frenetic search by the FBI for Stevenson. Investigators learned that a civilian employee of the Defense Department's Land Warfare Laboratory, physicist George Bert Stevenson, had been to Panama for several days coincidental with the date on the bill of sale produced by Gutenberg. George Bert Stevenson accounted for all of his time in Panama, named every individual with whom he associated, spent no time away from the site of his business, and, somewhat mystified, said that he had never been known as Verlin or Berlin Stevenson (agents suspected that possibly Swedes translated the B to a V and Stevenson at some point in his career perhaps spent time in the German city). But the only connection that George Bert Stevenson had with the fiction created by Gutenberg lay in a coincident surname.

With a confession of sorts from Reindolph, the Swedish police now arrested both Gutenberg and Axelsson in June, 1970. Neither were strangers to the officials; Gutenberg had served three years and six months starting in 1962 for "aggravated fraud and misappropriation," and Axelsson had been arrested and fined for the distribution of pornography in 1962. Reindolph on his guilty plea was sentenced by West German courts to a year's term in May, 1970, but in September of the same year he was deported to Montreal.

The Canadian-Swedish connection, like the affair of Marvin Karger and the fences, tantalized the investigators who studied the Morgan Guaranty caper. It was another instance where the information and leads stopped just short of a direct link into the upper echelons of organized crime. Members of the Joint Strike Force saw in the pattern of distribution a consistent parallel to the traffic in pornography. The key figure was believed to be Gus Cangiano, a genuine wise guy. Cangiano ran his business from a Brooklyn appliance shop. He supplied stolen credit cards, and furnished false identifications to thieves who looted the New York area airports during the 1960s and he was known as a major dealer in both securities and porn. But convinced though they were, the law enforcement agents could not bridge the gap between retailers such as Hite, Reindolph, and company and the mob. And at the other end of the chain they were similarly frustrated by the chasm between The Person and the mob.

VIII
The M and M Boys
South of the Border

While European financial institutions with their misunderstood reputation for confidentiality attracted action by some hot paper peddlers, other cognoscenti of the illegal concentrated on places closer to home. The Bahamas, for example, had long been a free-fire zone for criminal coups. Some norteamericanos harbored stereotypes of Latin Americans; they were inefficient, ignorant, and easily corrupted. From that ill-conceived seed, a pair of U.S. sharpies tried to harvest a Morgan Guaranty piece south of the border.

The plot began with an unworldly dupe, Xavier Cardenas, a Mexican-born, naturalized American citizen, who had labored for twenty-one years at the River Rouge, Michigan, plant of the Ford Motor Company. Classified by Ford as a "quality-control lab engineer," Xavier Cardenas earned just enough to support his wife and six children in a style that fell well below the more accelerated forms of conspicuous consumption.

In pursuit of an extra dollar, Xavier Cardenas manufactured for himself a number of identities, albeit retaining the same name. He kept his employment at Ford a secret from some of his acquaintances, coming on instead as a man of Mexican citizenship who spent much of his time in Detroit arranging affairs of import and export. And on his fairly frequent visits back to Mexico Xavier Cardenas remained silent about his actual occupation in the United States. He conveyed the impression that any propositions to buy or sell north of the border would find Cardenas a valuable asset.

It wasn't all talk either, for Xavier Cardenas managed to paper some of his ambitions. He passed out business cards for the "Xaco Corporation, Importers and Exporters Worldwide." He wrote letters on stationery with the Xaco name emblazoned on the paper. The address of the corporation was the same as his home. Xaco involved itself in a potpourri of enterprises. Cardenas attempted to ship canned Mexican delicacies to the U.S., offered to export American-made earthmoving equipment to his former homeland, proposed to broker tons of sulphur needed in Mexico. None of them ever got off the paper, however. In the closing months of 1969, Xavier Cardenas had already been through bankruptcy court once. He even had a run-in with the Detroit cops for allegedly lifting some steel from a railroad yard in order to make improvements around his home. U.S. Customs in Texas almost jailed Cardenas when inspectors caught him toting a dozen bottles of untaxed tequila north of the border to his Detroit compadres. Now, in November, Xavier Cardenas had been possessed by a new vision to turn a profit. He fantasized a cigar factory in Mexico. In hopes of finding backers he visited the offices of Sidney Solomon, an investment counselor, or more precisely a money-broker. Solomon, a Canadian citizen from Windsor, Ontario, just across the river from Detroit, rented office space on the second floor of a building in Southfield, a suburb of the Motor City. Downstairs from Solomon's place was a branch office of the National Bank of Southfield.

The Ford quality-control lab engineer, in his fractionated English, was in the process of spelling out the romance of cigar manufacturing when the party was joined by a third man, Melvin Markowitz. A builder of homes in Detroit, Toledo, Canton, and other Midwestern towns, he lived only a few blocks from the offices of Sidney Solomon. A World War II veteran, father of two, and a jogger, he occasionally paused to pass the time of day at Solomon's; Solomon had in the past located financing for Markowitz projects. Cardenas was slightly nonplused to find his cigar manufacturing balloon punctured by the appearance of this oddly dressed stranger. "I look at him in a sweatshirt but Sidney Solomon, he says, he's okay." Cardenas struggled manfully to maintain his posture as a serious investor with a solid base in Mexico City. But the cigar dream blew away in the smoke of casual conversation. The newcomer grandly appropriated several of the sample cigars brought to the conference by Cardenas.

However, a short time later, the would-be cigar factory impresario received a telephone call late one afternoon. The call actually awakened Cardenas, for he served his Ford time on the 4 A.M. to noon shift and usually went to bed when he arrived home. The voice announced itself as "Marvin" and asked if Cardenas were interested in making some money.

"I answered yes, of course. I am in debt," said Cardenas during his subsequent days in court. He was told to meet his new acquaintance Melvin Markowitz at a restaurant called Skandia.

At the appointed place, Cardenas and Markowitz rendezvoused. "Can you dispose of some documents in Mexico," is how Cardenas remembered the builder's opening gambit. "I don't think so," was the response. Markowitz pressed on. "If you really want to make money, I want to get in touch with you, because you are wasting your time with Solomon. You have been to see him for three months and it has never produced anything."

According to Cardenas, Markowitz professed a desire to meet him, "Because he has a beautiful business for me so we can make a lot of money. Well, I owes lots of money. I am in debt, I said, 'Beautiful.'"

Further conversations between Markowitz and Cardenas ensued at a Holiday Inn and a Howard Johnson's in Detroit, as the home builder unraveled his money-making skein. Markowitz put on the table reasons why it was necessary to "dispose of documents" in Mexico—to avoid payment of taxes. Not only were taxes too high in the U.S., but Markowitz and friends expected to invest the proceeds from the document sales in Mexico.

During the session at the Holiday Inn, Markowitz revealed exactly the type of document to be sold. "He told me that some friends, they have some Treasury notes from the U.S. government. And it was better than gold and they want to sell it in Mexico.

"I told him I had never seen any type of document of that kind or was not familiar. I have friends in Mexico that might be able to do something, however." Markowitz explained that while he did not actually have a Treasury bill to show to Cardenas he would secure a copy. And at a subsequent discussion at Howard Johnson's on Grand Boulevard, Markowitz passed over to Cardenas a photocopy of a Treasury bill. In return for his help in negotiating the instrument, Cardenas was promised 5 percent of the proceeds, and another 5 percent would be tendered to his Mexican associates who assisted in the operation.

Xavier Cardenas had never seen the actual Treasury bill, only a photocopy. Others, unknown to Cardenas, had been approached and actually tried to negotiate the certificate. During the early winter months that Melvin Markowitz was in discussion with Xavier Cardenas on the sale of "documents" in Mexico, he visited James T. Stone, then bank manager and assistant cashier of the National Bank of Southfield. James Stone knew Sidney Solomon, the upstairs tenant, well; Melvin Markowitz, however, had no account at the bank; he merely cashed an occasional check there.

On this mid-February call on James Stone, Melvin Markowitz asked if the Southfield bank would cash a $100,000 Treasury bill that he held for an unidentified friend. Markowitz told Stone that in the event he could not receive all of the money immediately, he was willing to accept $10,000 up front until the total could be collected.

Stone said that his bank was not in a position to handle such a transaction but it could be worked through a correspondent bank, City National Bank. As a first step, Stone telephoned the appropriate officer at City National, read him the number of a Treasury bill proffered by Markowitz. The City National man scanned the hot list, called the expert at the local Federal Reserve Bank. All was in order. He then told Stone that the paper appeared to be properly negotiable. If brought to the downtown Detroit offices of City National, the T bill would be accepted.

Markowitz invited James Stone to accompany him to the City National Bank where the Southfield manager was known. Stone was agreeable and transportation downtown was furnished by a friend of Markowitz, Marvin Mulligan, in a Cadillac Eldorado. While the double M's sat in the parked Caddy, outside of City National, James Stone entered the bank and approached the gentlemen in charge of government securities. A call was placed to the manager of

Treasury Issues Department at the Detroit Federal Reserve Bank. This time, hearing approximately the same number for a T bill as had been submitted earlier that day, the fed officer did not even bother to look at his hot list. He reported no problem with the bill.

There was, however, a problem so far as the small huddle of bankers at City National were concerned. "Normally," said James Stone when he appeared in court later, "you don't cash a bill that is not matured and you don't want cash [meaning currency]." The bankers all felt the deal seemed a "bit queer."

As a minimal protection for themselves, they agreed to accept the Treasury bill but not in a simple exchange of greenbacks for certificate. Instead, they offered to credit the National Bank of Southfield with the $95,000 or so due. Southfield could then issue a cashier's check made out to Melvin Markowitz. That of course required Markowitz to come forward and sign for the money. If something went awry he could not simply say that James Stone had made some egregious error in connecting him with the Treasury bill. Melvin Markowitz thanked Stone for his efforts but refused to go ahead with a cashier's check arrangement. He pocketed his Treasury bill. He and Marvin Mulligan dropped off Stone back at the National Southfield branch.

In late February Markowitz telephoned Cardenas to order reservations for three people on a flight to Mexico City the following day. The liaison with the Mexican banking authorities protested that he could not take off quite so abruptly. He had to make peace with his supervisor at the River Rouge plant. But he agreed to be ready in a few days and Markowitz instructed him to secure three places on a plane to Mexico City. The tickets were to be reserved for Markowitz, Cardenas, and a "Frank Smith."

However, Cardenas reminded the builder that passport and Customs control would not accept just any name, so the reservation was then made in the name of "Frank Mulligan." At the airport, the third man appeared. His name was actually Marvin Mulligan, the chap who first telephoned a sleepy Cardenas back in November. Marvin Mulligan was a tall, handsome man in his late thirties, in the home siding business. He had a felony conviction on his record from a while back. "He was," said an Assistant U.S. Attorney, "nothing less than a standup hood."

Cardenas had arranged for tourist-class tickets but at the airport Melvin Markowitz grandly revised the order of march; the party would ride in the front of the airplane. "When you are with us, you get to be first-class." The big spender charged all of the fares to his American Express card, to be paid on the extended-payment plan, over a three-month period.

The flight to Mexico in the first-class cabin was a convivial one. When the jet paused in San Antonio, Markowitz handed Cardenas a $20 bill, after the latter mentioned how much his chums over the border enjoyed a pull on scotch whiskey. Cardenas bought two bottles.

Between four and six of Cardenas's friends greeted the plane at the Mexico City airport. Markowitz signed everyone in at the Maria Isabel Hotel. The group bunked down in a junior suite and the small-scale fiesta continued. Among those present were two local export-import merchants, Andres and David Fernandez, and an architect, José Manuel Coeto Pineda.

The central topic of conversation was the wealthy norteamericanos who had come to Mexico to invest in real estate and construction. For them to open up their account, it was explained to the Mexicans, it would be necessary to arrange for redemption of a particular piece of paper. From inside his shirt, Marvin Mulligan drew forth a wrinkled

$100,000 certificate which he passed to Melvin Markowitz who then tossed it on a table for the Mexicans to examine. "You guys ever see such a big amount as this?" bragged Markowitz. The Americans remarked that the Mexican businessmen undoubtedly dealt with local banking officials. If this paper transaction went through, said an expansive Markowitz, he would produce another $10,000,000. Several individuals present in the suite thought they saw a brief case packed with paper similar in nature to the one on the table.

In the morning, the newly recruited aides of Mulligan and Markowitz set out for the banks. An architect named Amdo Moga was given a copy of the Treasury bill, another copy was in the hands of Andres and David Fernandez, while Xavier Cardenas had possession of the original. The Fernandez brothers went to the Hacienda, the popular name for the National Treasury of Mexico, which also performed the functions of Federal Reserve Banks in the U.S. The brothers were informed that the Hacienda could not negotiate a U.S. Treasury bill; the Hacienda simply did not deal with the banking needs of individuals. They were told to go to the ordinary commercial banks of the city. Xavier Cardenas selected the local branch of the U.S. First National City Bank. Something in the approach made by Cardenas to a bank officer aroused suspicion in the executive. He discouraged Cardenas from pursuing the matter further at that particular bank and Cardenas headed back to the Maria Isabel. But before he left the premises of First National City, the alert official secured the number of the bill, 1017056A, and teletyped the description to the New York offices of First National City.

At the Maria Isabel, Melvin Markowitz abandoned his good-time face: "He was mad," said Cardenas during the subsequent trial. "I was supposed to have a connection with the government and a bank. But I was just a waste of time and money. I was supposed to dispose of this note immediately." Cardenas pleaded for another chance. "If you don't dispose of this note tomorrow," said Markowitz, "we are going to the Bahamas and to hell with you."

Cardenas gave his associates a pep-talk with visions of a weekend savoring the pleasures of Acapulco, if the note could be negotiated. Architect Coeto remarked that he had a friend, one Señor Damiean who held a position as a purchasing agent for the government. Undoubtedly he had the right connections. On the following day, Coeto and Cardenas met with Damiean at the Banco del Atlantico. The manager of the institution informed them that a Mexican-owned bank would not negotiate such a piece of paper without permission from the Bank of Mexico, and that would take several days. However, stockbrokers in Mexico could handle the deal more easily by operating through non-Mexican banks. The bank manager hailed Señor Roberto Hernandez, a broker, who happened to be passing.

The broker allowed that he was in a position to play middleman in such a transaction. Coeto and Cardenas agreed to meet Roberto Hernandez at Banco del Atlantico later in the day to receive the proceeds on the Treasury bill. Cardenas removed the certificate from his jacket pocket and handed it to Roberto Hernandez.

"No receipt was necessary," said Hernandez, when Cardenas requested one. "We use the word as the contract." The broker took the Treasury bill to his office where he busied himself for several hours. He then went to the local stock exchange for the purpose of discharging his normal duties and to fulfill his mission at a U.S. bank with offices in the stock exchange building, the First National City Bank. At that institution word had already come back from New York on certificate 1017056A. When the broker broached the subject of the Treasury bill, in short order the Mexican police arrived at First National City to question Hernandez. Also summoned to the bank was a Mr. Miller, who was described as the legal attaché at the U.S. embassy but in reality was an FBI agent. He accepted custody of the T bill from Roberto Hernandez.

Meanwhile, the offices of Banco del Atlantico were closing their doors. Coeto and Cardenas finally were forced to leave. They telephoned to Damiean who explained the turn of events. Andres Fernandez was also advised by his friends that the T bill was stolen. He relayed the facts to David Fernandez, who had waited with Markowitz in a cafe while Marvin Mulligan rested an achy back in the Maria Isabel junior suite.

On receipt of the news, Xavier Cardenas hesitated not at all. He rushed immediately to the U.S. embassy to explain his part in the affair. The Mexican police, meanwhile, arrested the pair of yanquis at the Maria Isabel without exhibiting any warrant. Markowitz and Mulligan were subjected to a disagreeable interrogation that did not recognize any right to counsel during the interviews. Subsequently, Melvin Markowitz and Marvin Mulligan were trundled onto a night plane that carried them to Houston, Texas, where FBI agents took them into custody. No arrest warrant was shown there either.

After Mexican police and the U.S. embassy had interviewed Xavier Cardenas, he was loaded aboard a jet to Detroit. FBI agents greeted him at the airport also. The Mexican nationals were all absolved of any guilt in the enterprise. Later, U.S. Attorneys in Detroit spent many hours on the telephone to the U.S. embassy in a major effort to get the Mexican citizens to appear in court as prosecution witnesses.

When Markowitz arrived back in Detroit, the feds sought a confession from him. Assistant U.S. Attorney Arnold Schulman said, "I told his lawyer that if Markowitz

would plead guilty and talk, he'd get an eighteen-month
sentence. After six months he'd walk. But I got nowhere
with Markowitz. He rambled on about everything but he
refused to cooperate."

The U.S. Attorney's office spent a considerable amount
of time interviewing James Stone. He would not be the
first bank employee to have engaged in an operation that
would assist in the negotiation of stolen securities. The
feds pondered whether he might not be a partner to the attempt in Detroit to cash the bill. Twice Stone agreed to
undertake polygraph tests. His spontaneous willingness to
be hooked up to the machines convinced the authorities
that he had essentially told the truth. No actual polygraphs
were made, however. Stone's testimony about Markowitz's
behavior when the T bill was brought to the City National
Bank in Detroit wiped out a defense contention that Markowitz had been so innocent and so determined to be certain the bill was legally negotiable that he had checked it
out with the U.S. banks. A mystery that neither the investigation nor the trial cleared up was how the U.S. financial
institutions failed to spot 1017056A as stolen. One theory
held that a pair of numbers became transposed during the
reading of the serial to the Federal Reserve Bank official.
And when a second call about the bill arrived, because of
the similarity to the earlier description, the executive assumed it was the same item and did not bother to check it
out again. Another hypothesis contended that the T bill
shown by Markowitz in Detroit was not the one presented
in Mexico and the first piece was simply not yet on a hot
list.

The trial in Detroit at times looked like a pilot for a situation comedy on TV. At one of the preliminary hearings a
judge looked at a female Assistant U.S. Attorney and
asked, "Who is this young lady?"

"Miss Marshall from the Department of Justice Task

Force," she answered. The judge: "Marshall? They sure have improved this staff up there."

Melvin Markowitz wanted his trial severed from Marvin Mulligan on the grounds that his "Co-defendant is a man with a long history of anti-social conduct including but not limited to lengthy durations in the penitentiary." The brief further argued that Mulligan's presentation of himself at the trial will "embarrass the defendant and will blind the jury to the evidence." Defense moved for a dismissal on grounds that the third person to the theft (The Person) had not been identified in the indictment. The judge refused to consider that argument, which would eliminate prosecution of most cases of illicit stock and bond sales. Defense asked to exclude any statements by Xavier Cardenas on the basis of the Miranda rule; his legal counsel was not present during the interrogation. But Miranda clearly covers only an individual who confesses to his own part in a crime, not anyone who claims to be an unwitting accomplice.

Throughout the trial, attorneys and witnesses bumbled the names of the principal parties. Confusion arose over Andres Fernandez, David Fernandez, Roberto Hernandez, and Xavier Cardenas. Nor did the speakers do much better with the Anglos; the double M's of Melvin Markowitz and Marvin Mulligan led to several scenes in which Clyde Woody, a flamboyant Houston defense attorney for the former, was corrected by Neil Fink, lawyer for Mulligan, as Woody had undertaken a sonorous defense of the wrong name.

Xavier Cardenas, dressed in a cheap suit, gesticulating and tripping over his tongue, slipped on pronouns and perverted normal English syntax. Under cross-examination he admitted to some inconsistencies between the original statements he gave the FBI and to the court. FBI notes showed that Cardenas said he checked on the T bill's legitimacy at the National Bank of Detroit. In his tale to the jury he said he did not have possession of the bill until Mexico City.

In a routine effort to impugn Cardenas, the defense insinuated to the jury that Cardenas's credibility was suspect because in return for his testimony the government agreed not to prosecute him. The Ford employee argued he was never under arrest and therefore was not a witness for the prosecution because of a bargain struck with the government. Cardenas insisted that of his own volition he had asked to see the FBI immediately upon his return to the States. The appearance of the two FBI men as he cleared Customs, said Cardenas, he accepted as a very speedy fulfillment of his request. "They gave me my rights but they never handcuffed me up. I watched the FBI every Sunday [on TV] and the first thing they do is put you in handcuffs so that's why I told you I was not arrested." However, his source of information had misled him. Agents from Detroit told the court that they had distinctly informed Cardenas that he was under arrest.

The Mexican citizens who testified at the trial, Roberto Hernandez, David Fernandez and José Coeto, all experienced some difficulty with the meaning of some questions. Words such as "event" and "maturity" puzzled the Mexicans. The court misunderstood several of the answers. Architect Coeto recounted how he waited in the Banco del Atlantico for news from Roberto Hernandez. Coeto said the bank was closing and he was getting a loan. Defense pounced on possible motivation for Coeto's testimony; that he had suffered some financial loss because the T bill was not negotiated. Only after several minutes of back and forth was it discovered that Coeto had meant that as everyone departed from the bank he was "getting alone."

The counselors for the defense asked for a mistrial because the government did not try hard enough to bring a

critical witness, the brother of David Fernandez, Andres.
Defense had obtained a copy of the interrogation of
Andres in Mexico. He said, according to this interview,
that it was Xavier Cardenas who possessed the T bill and
in fact had flashed it at him while they rode in an elevator.
This version contradicted the stories told by the other witnesses actually at the trial. The U.S. Attorney's representatives suggested that the discrepancy arose from Andres's
inability to understand English and that something was
garbled in translation of his account. Furthermore, the
government told the judge it had done everything in its
power to get Andres to appear in Detroit. But the business
that he operated in partnership with David Fernandez
could not afford to have both brothers away at the same
time. The court was respectfully reminded that subpoenas
upon foreign nationals living outside of the U.S. have no
power. The motion for a mistrial was rejected.

A dapper Marvin Mulligan exercised his privilege to
remain silent during his trial. But an almost equally well-
dressed Melvin Markowitz, in what an Assistant U.S. Attorney called a "$200 suit," pleaded his defense. He ex-
plained that Sidney Solomon was engaged in a scheme to
invest $300,000,000 in Mexico through Xavier Cardenas
and his acquaintances. When Solomon fell ill with pneu-
monia, the money-broker asked his friend Markowitz to
represent him in Mexico and secure from the Hacienda
the necessary paper commitment from the financial pow-
ers.

According to Markowitz, while he and Cardenas drove
to Detroit after a visit to Solomon, then recuperating at his
Windsor, Ontario, home, Cardenas produced the T bill and
asked the builder "if I could accommodate him, if I could
get it cashed for him." As a good fellow Markowitz paid
his call on James Stone at the National Bank of Southfield.
He said he refused the cashier's check from the City Na-

tional Bank because he might have problems with the Internal Revenue Service if he endorsed such a check. After all, the money belonged to Xavier Cardenas. However, even if Markowitz had received cash, City National's records would still have recorded, for the benefit of the IRS, a payment of better than $95,000 to one Melvin Markowitz. Markowitz steadfastly insisted that in Detroit he gave the Treasury bill back to Cardenas and never saw it again.

Markowitz was asked how Marvin Mulligan came to join the excursion to Mexico. It seemed that while at the offices of his insurance agent, Mulligan, a casual acquaintance whom Markowitz had not seen for five or six months, appeared. While chatting, Markowitz mentioned his forthcoming trip to Mexico. Mulligan said, "I've never been to Mexico."

"If you want to come, come on," invited the builder who generously advanced his companion a first-class ticket through the medium of his American Express card.

Cross-examination of Markowitz revealed his business was a leaky ship: a $70,000 debt threatened to sink the entire enterprise. The prosecution chipped away at the credibility of Markowitz: Why had he and Mulligan chosen to remain outside the City National Bank in the Cadillac while James Stone met with officials by himself? The U.S. Attorney insinuated that the pair wished to keep their faces and identities secret in the event the bill proved hot. The prosecutor scoffed at the circumstances that supposedly led to Mulligan fastening himself to the Mexico-bound party. Markowitz parried with a claim that Mulligan was supposed to pay him for the air fare, but there was no tangible evidence of any recompense from Mulligan.

In his final appeal to the jury, Clyde Woody, Markowitz's lawyer, resorted to a teary tune: "Either you are going to exonerate this man . . . or you are going to destroy his life, essentially because a conviction is what that will do. It will destroy him and his family."

It was a standard defense number, but Judge Thomas Thornton reacted like a critic who is suddenly asked to consider an amateur actor in the light of Laurence Olivier. "We adjourn now until two o'clock," said the judge. "But before adjourning, any verdict that you return as jurors, your verdict isn't going to ruin the life of anybody. The testimony in this case that brought about the verdict might have an impact on anybody, but not your verdict."

It was an astonishing view of the matter, since Markowitz and Mulligan faced substantial prison sentences if found guilty. Neil Fink immediately protested on behalf of his client, Mulligan, and asked for a mistrial. Judge Thornton refused to admit that his remarks could have prejudiced the jury.

In his speech, Clyde Woody also instructed the jury, "You can tell whether a man or woman is not telling the truth because . . . he's probably going to squirm around in his chair." Indeed, the voluble Xavier Cardenas did bounce about while testifying. However, William Jones, the senior prosecutor, quickly picked up on the body language of tellers of fiction. He offered his own clues to liars. "The mouth gets dry," observed Jones, a pointed reference to what seemed to be gallons of water consumed by visibly sweating Melvin Markowitz while he was on the witness stand.

The jury brought in guilty verdicts against both men. Judge Thornton, who saw nothing ruinous in any verdict, sentenced both men to serve five-year terms in federal prisons. As the courtroom emptied, prosecuting attorney Arnold Schulman could not resist whispering to Clyde Woody, "Eighteen months, eighteen months," to remind the defense lawyer of the bargain once offered to Woody's client.

The jury, said Arnold Schulman in retrospect, saw Xavier Cardenas as an engine of blundering ambition. The attempts by the defense to erode Cardenas's veracity only heightened the judgment that he was not smart enough to have masterminded any plot to dispose of a Treasury bill. Nor could much stock be placed in a tale that Cardenas, as Markowitz said, had been engaged in a $300,000,000 investment proposition with the mysterious Sidney Solomon. No sharp financier could possibly have trusted the fumbling visionary to carry through a monster investment plan.

Solomon was a mystery to the prosecution even after the trial. He was the one individual who could have supported Markowitz's version of why he journeyed to Mexico. But the defense never even subpoenaed Solomon; in fact at one point they suggested to Cardenas that it was Solomon who gave the Treasury bill to him. Cardenas denied that allegation.

Although Markowitz insisted he never saw the Treasury bill in Mexico City, two witnesses, Cardenas and David Fernandez, testified that they saw the bill go from safekeeping next to the chest of Marvin Mulligan to the hand of Melvin Markowitz on several occasions. José Coeto even saw Markowitz retrieve the item from his brief case. In an appeal of the case Woody sought to capitalize, Texas-style, upon the nature of these witnesses. He implied in the Sixth Circuit Court of Appeals in Cincinnati before Judge Edwards that his Texas colleagues would never take the word of a bunch of Mexicans.

The Sixth Circuit Court of Appeals happened to be populated by judges who placed principles of law above bias. The neck and face of Judge Edwards on hearing the slur on the Mexicans registered boil red. The appeals were all turned down leaving Markowitz and Mulligan to serve their time.

The Detroit Task Force is at least partially convinced that the Americans carried other securities with them to Mexico. The feds remembered Markowitz had boasted of $10,000,000 more, and the testimony about a brief case with what appeared to be more securities. Nothing turned up in the search of the room and one theory is that after the first futile day trying to cash the Treasury bill, the other materials were mailed back to the United States to reduce liability in the event of trouble.

There was one other item of note that did not make the trial record. Miller, the FBI agent listed as the legal attaché to the embassy (it's a common practice at U.S. legations in several countries), enjoyed a comfortable liaison with the Mexican police. He was permitted to personally search the rooms at the Maria Isabel. Miller also secured from the Maria Isabel a copy of the toll telephone calls made from the suite occupied by Markowitz and Mulligan. One call went to a toy and novelty store in Brooklyn that belonged to a tough guy who had done a stretch for armed robbery as a member of a Coney Island gang called "Holdup, Inc." The proprietor of the store also operated a bar frequented by people associated with organized crime. But that was all that the FBI could make of the matter. The owner of the toy and novelty store blandly said that many people called his place and he couldn't remember any messages from Mexico. Neither of the two convicted men offered any information on the nature of the call to Brooklyn. The investigation could not add any links to the chain that began October 16, 1969.

IX
Other Foreign Affairs

The rush to negotiate pieces outside of the continental limits of the United States undoubtedly owed much to the logical premise that the further knowledge must travel, the better the chance that somewhere along the line the communication would be filed and forgotten. The thesis gripped not only the casual securities swindlers such as Cuomo and Marchese, Reindolph and the M and M boys; it was also an axiom with some of the more experienced salesmen of hot paper.

On November 1, 1969, detectives at the Bond and Forgery Squad in New York City received a telephone call from the Royal Canadian Mounted Police in Toronto that asked about a New Yorker who went by the name of Michael C. Van Beuren. The Mounties had detained the man at the airport and he appeared to possess in the neighborhood of $180,000 in warrants (rights to buy shares) of Leasco Data Processing Equipment Corporation.

The name Michael C. Van Beuren signified nothing to

the New York detectives but the description of the American added up to a very familiar figure, Emanuel Lester. "He looked like Dick Tracy's old nemesis, Prune Face," said Joe Leahy. Manny Lester was a close associate of veteran securities cheat Peter Crosby. They were inseparable except when federal officials intervened because of their ways with stocks, bonds, and other papers of financial value. Lester filled several cards in the file on criminal indictments in the Southern District of New York. The Securities and Exchange Commission as part of its advice to the newly formed Bond and Forgery unit in New York City advised the cops to pay special attention to any rumor that Manny Lester might be on the prowl in the New York City jurisdiction.

"On one occasion, we were going over some documents that appeared to be part of a swindle," recalls Joe Leahy. "We were assured everything was legitimate and then suddenly I see the signature of Emanuel Lester at the bottom of one page. That's the biggest fucking crook in the world, I yell."

On the basis of the physical description of the middle-aged Van Beuren, the New York cops rushed a photograph of Lester out to the airport. An obliging pilot agreed to hand over the picture to a Mountie in Toronto. The suspicions of the New Yorkers proved to be as valid as Lester was crooked.

Properly identified, Emanuel Lester was confined for close to a year in a Canadian prison for attempting to sell the stolen Leasco warrants to Canada. Having worked his way through three defense counselors appointed by the Ontario Supreme Court, he eventually went on trial charged with unlawful possession of roughly $175,000 in Leasco Data Processing Equipment warrants. In addition to these charges which rose out of his initial arrest, Lester was also accused of unlawful possession of one hundred shares of preferred stock for Western Union Telegraph and possession of a Diner's Club credit card that belonged actually to Michael C. Van Beuren.

The jury brought in a guilty verdict on most of the charges (there was a separate one for each block of warrants in his hands) and the American received a four-year sentence. Since he had waited to be tried for a year in jail, Lester earned his release shortly thereafter. He returned to the U.S. where the feds promptly put the arm on him for a number of other stock frauds. In 1974, apparently discouraged by his prospects, Manny Lester committed suicide.

When the Mounties took Lester into custody, they quite naturally searched his effects. Stashed among his other ill-gotten valuables they discovered four pieces from the Morgan Guaranty Trust robbery, a $1,000,000 note, a $100,000 piece, and two $50,000 ones. The officials in Canada decided that it would be difficult to prove that Lester actually had knowledge of the theft and was guilty of illegal possession. He had not yet had an opportunity to demonstrate criminal knowledge by an attempt to negotiate them either.

More than three months after the last of the T bills had reached their maturity date of April 16, 1970, Executive Vice President Henry Rohlf at the Morgan Guaranty offices was notified that a Swiss newspaper had picked up a story from *Corriere Della Sera,* a Milan paper which had mentioned the Morgan Guaranty theft and had indicated that a Milanese attorney, Federico Gobi, recently deposited three $100,000 Treasury bills in the Banco Populare Svizzera at Lugano, Switzerland.

Rohlf immediately called the FBI offices in New York and the Bureau put together what it could about the Italian-Swiss transaction.

Federico Gobi, a lawyer of no disrepute, walked into the

Banco Populare Svizzera where he had done business before, and asked to see Director Mahler. He was unfortunately away for the moment, but Vice Director Emilio Jecchi and Assistant Bank Director Flavio Pedrazzoli placed themselves at Signor Gobi's service. The Italian lawyer submitted three U.S. Treasury bills, each worth $100,000 and which had matured on April 9, 1970. Gobi accepted a receipt, asked for nothing in advance, and left the bank.

About an hour later, Gobi returned and this time Director Mahler was available. Gobi mentioned the deposit of the Treasury bills and in the course of his remarks admitted to having carried the bills from Italy to Switzerland on his person. Director Mahler, somewhat surprised, pointed out to the attorney that this was a serious crime under Italian laws. It amounted to smuggling currency out of the country. Rico Gobi expressed ignorance of the rules. "Much to our surprise," said Mahler, "he answered that since the bills represented a foreign currency he had not felt that he was taking any risks."

Signor Gobi proposed that he avoid any future jeopardy by mailing more Treasury bills directly to the bank. An official rejected the scheme on the grounds that the customs officials would screen outgoing letters that were directed to bank officials. However, he was willing to receive materials mailed directly to his home address. Swiss bankers and Swiss laws cut a very nice line for their customers. Any client who transgresses against the Swiss regulations suffers immediate exposure by the fiduciary officials, and the courts deal harshly with him. But any customer who stays within the Swiss codes can trample the currency laws of any other nation without fear of exposure or punishment by the Swiss.

Unhappily for Rico Gobi, the Banco Populare Svizzera had on file Swiss bankers' circular letter 4112 dated October 27, 1969, and it carried the numbers of the three Treasury bills received from Gobi as stolen. Several days after his return to Milan, Rico Gobi received a call from Lugano informing him that the items he deposited were among those filched from a New York bank and would he please come to Lugano to straighten out the matter. At first Rico Gobi told his long-distance callers that he would be delighted to accommodate them.

A short while later, however, Gobi reneged. He informed the Swiss that he now knew that he had been conned, that he had received the bills from a total stranger and had no desire to face the Swiss authorities under the circumstances. Inevitably, the Italian police visited Rico Gobi for an explanation of the request for extradition by the Swiss. Gobi's tale to the local investigators differed sharply from that he gave to Director Mahler.

Shortly before his ill-fated trip to Lugano, Rico Gobi said he took a telephone call from a man who requested the Milanese attorney to negotiate some securities. Gobi received some photocopies of the items and to him they appeared authentic. Except that a photocopy indicates what a Treasury bill looks like, such identification is near worthless. Like U.S. currency, special paper is used in the manufacture of Treasury bills and its presence would be extremely difficult to detect in a photocopy. The quality of the engraving, likewise, would be indeterminate in a photocopy. That, however, was counselor Gobi's story.

Gobi said that the individual who mailed the photocopies said he was prepared to negotiate another $1.7 million of securities if Gobi could accommodate him with the first transaction. Acting on instructions, Gobi said he kept a rendezvous in Lugano, at a fountain next to Innovazione, a department store. There a "small fat man wearing dark glasses" passed over to Gobi the three $100,000 Treasury notes. He explained that it was necessary to employ an intermediary because otherwise the

"principal might be exposed and this is money out of the
Nixon campaign fund." The Italian police were most un-
impressed by the account, however ingeniously it served
to make the Milanese innocent of transgression. The story
that he received the T bills in Lugano obviously absolved
Gobi of having violated currency laws for carrying the bills
over the border. What is astonishing, however, is the reference to the Nixon campaign fund, almost two years before
the 1972 campaign finance laws went into effect and the
break-in at the Democratic Party headquarters at Wa-
tergate, which led to the disclosures about financial irregularities in the 1972 election. What seemed like an ex-
traordinarily farfetched piece of fiction held within it at
least a prophecy of the way things would be done, if they
had not already been done that way.

During the first year after the theft of the Treasury bills,
pieces continued to pop up outside the United States. In
August of 1970, Louis Amhof, a Swiss citizen, deposited
for cash a $100,000 Treasury bill numbered 1017486A in
the Schweizerische Volksbank in Basel. The note, said
Amhof, was the property of his firm, Formo Company, and
the money from redemption was to be placed in the account of another Amhof enterprise, Fombia Finance Co.

The security was presented to Banque Populaire Suisse,
Basel, the collection agent for the Volksbank. It was then
transmitted to Brown Brothers Harriman and Co., which
acted as the U.S. agent for the Swiss bank. The T bill was
accompanied by the required "certificate of ownership,"
form PD 1071 that carried data about Louis Amhof and
both of his companies. In November of 1970, said Volksbank executive Josef Ehrler, "We were informed that the
securities in question had been stolen and neither it nor
the money would be returned." Ehrler, in making a statement to the U.S. authorities looking into the incident said,
"The enclosed form PD 1071 shows clearly that the bank

handled the transaction in good faith and therefore did not keep records of it. I can certify that the procedure for requesting payment is normal, regular business practice of the bank. Since no records were kept, none can be shown here."

Presumably, the Schweizerische Volksbank had somewhere in its files the same Swiss bankers' circular letter 4112 that alerted executives at Banco Populare Svizzera in Lugano about the nature of the ownership of the bills presented by Rico Gobi. The people at the Volksbank appear to be guilty of negligent handling. The absence of records indicates that the desire of Swiss financiers to turn an extra franc is a definite asset to thieves of money instruments. Why it required roughly three months for word that the piece was stolen property to reach the Schweizerische Volksbank is another curiosity.

The Americans who investigated the case determined that Louis Amhof had been associated with three other men and indictments were returned against not only Amhof, but Jerome Fields, a naturalized American born in Austria, and two West Germans, Charles Lembertz and Herman Langnas. Of the quartet, only Fields and Langnas, who were unlucky enough to return to the United States, went on trial. Lembertz and Amhof stayed out of the U.S. and became officially listed as fugitives from justice.

Jerome Fields, Charles Lembertz, and Herman Langnas met in Torremolinos in the summer of 1970. Fields apparently introduced the West Germans to one another and he also acquainted them with another American by the name of James Stevenson. The government in its case against Langnas contended that it was Stevenson who carried the T bill to Basel where Langnas brought it to Amhof for negotiation. Langnas pleaded guilty through an interpreter and was put on probation for two years.

Fields, however, insisted that all he had contributed was

a series of introductions and played no role in any illegal transaction. The first trial resulted in a hung jury. Tried a second time before a judge by agreement of both prosecution and defense, Fields was declared not guilty.

Another $100,000 piece surfaced in the Dutch island of St. Martin in the Caribbean. In June of 1970, four men were accused of attempting to use the bill to secure a loan for use at the local gambling casino. The St. Martin bank had refused to redeem the bill and then the four men allegedly requested a $15,000 loan, using the bill as collateral. An Assistant U.S. Attorney flew to St. Martin to investigate the case. Indictments were returned but the government faced considerable difficulty in making a case. The problem was to produce proof that the defendants knew the item was stolen. There was an individual whom the U.S. Attorney thought might provide the necessary testimony but the informant decided not to cooperate. The indictments were dropped.

No arrests followed the recovery of another $500,000 piece, although the incident followed a bizarre trail. Some unidentified individuals approached a bank in Nassau, Bahamas, with a $500,000 Treasury bill in January, 1970. The Bahamas had served as a free zone for negotiators of stock swindles. The behavior of the Bahamian bank indicated why the underworld favored Nassau. Instead of checking to see if the bill had a legitimate parentage, the bank approached the local offices of a U.S. brokerage firm, Loeb Rhoades. That firm, however, refused to handle the piece. The Nassau bank then requested the National Bank of North America to negotiate the T bill for it. As a result, the piece was sent up to the U.S. for collection. Ironically, the bank to which it was presented was Morgan Guaranty Trust. Mrs. Janet Montague, an employee of the bank, received the piece and almost immediately recognized it as one of the items stolen three months earlier.

For her vigilance, Morgan Guaranty Trust rewarded Mrs. Montague with $1,500. Her pleasure was dampened by anti-Semitic remarks from a fellow employee who also mumbled that the Mafia knew how to handle people who interfered with their plans. When Mrs. Montague received some threatening telephone calls at home, FBI agents investigated. They did not discover any source for the phone messages. Agents shook the loudmouth in the office but he proved to be nothing more sinister than an empty bigot. He escaped with a severe reprimand from his employers and a warning from the Bureau. Mrs. Montague was left to enjoy her prize as best she could.

There were no arrests made in the Bahamas and no clues uncovered on the persons who had brought the $500,000 bill to the Bahamian bank.

None of the foreign affairs came close to offering a real lead for the FBI agents. Depending upon which country one dealt with, some details on the actual attempt to negotiate a piece might be supplied to the Bureau offices in New York, but there was no opportunity to do any investigating. Interpol, the well-publicized international police association, was useless except as a conduit for information. The organization is largely a paper operation that shies away from any real investigative work because of possible political implications. The frustration with the piece delivered to the Bahamian bank epitomized the situation so far as lawmen were concerned. The investigators could take very little credit for the recoveries; those were due to observant clerks. And the arrests, such as they were, did not get to the heart of the crime.

X

Monkey and Knobby's Caper

The foreign failures, as well as the unsuccessful tries by plumber Lester Spivak with Laidlaw & Company and Marvin Karger in Boston, were each due to an inability to cozen a bank or brokerage house and in Karger's case to the discovery of a number of negotiated T bills coming out of Brookline's Town Bank and Trust. Several other schemes collapsed because of the deadliest weapon in law enforcement, the informer.

Joseph De Rienzo, a 42-year-old native of Brooklyn, was at most a fringe member of organized crime. As a 14-year-old kid he was picked up for juvenile delinquency; he progressed to burglary of a store at age 17. Then he abandoned the muscular forms of crime for the devious ones. He worked as a bookmaker and a numbers runner, earning arrests for gambling in 1949 and 1964. For a time he almost made it as a soldier in the legions of Tommy Eboli, a.k.a. Tommy Ryan, a Brooklyn underboss who rose to preeminence in the Brooklyn gang hierarchy. Until Eboli was shot down in the street in 1972 after leaving what the tabloids call a tryst, his most celebrated public appearance had been in the 1950s when he leaped into the ring in Madison Square Garden and attempted to assault the referee for a decision against the Eboli-Ryan fighter Rocky Castellani.

In 1969, it had already been four or five years since Joe De Rienzo had contact with the rising star Eboli. He was still on speaking terms with an Eboli henchman, Tommy Agro, for whom he had done some bookmaking and shylock work. But mainly Joe De Rienzo wandered by himself along the edge between criminal behavior and legitimate conduct. He worked, for example, at an honest job as a letter carrier. But on the side, De Rienzo operated as a shylock, lending five dollars to associates in return for a payment of six dollars one week later, an interest rate of 20 percent per week. "I don't call that vigorish [a term applied both to a bookmaker's cut and a usurer's profit]," said De Rienzo once. "I see it as just appreciation for lending somebody money when they need it."

Mostly De Rienzo scrounged. "When I worked for the mob," he said, "I'd make maybe $25,000 or $30,000 in a year. I threw it away." Admittedly, fellows like De Rienzo have a tendency to exaggerate the size of their scores, but unquestionably De Rienzo squandered much of what he made on horses at Aqueduct race track. On at least one occasion, when in a bind, he tried to defraud a bank with a loan application that used a fellow letter carrier's name.

De Rienzo was by no means a Dicky the Dunce. He earned a high school equivalency diploma and he attended Brooklyn College for six months in 1955 when he was already 28. Married with four children, Joe De Rienzo bore a nine-inch scar on the left side of his neck and a tattoo, "In Memory of My Dear Father," on his right shoulder. He also carried the nickname of Monkey, for a simian resemblance discerned in some of his expressions.

In the autumn of 1969, with perhaps the melancholy of coming middle age or possibly on the lookout for a good thing, he began to frequent his old Brooklyn neighborhood, the East New York section, in whose warrens lived many of the minor functionaries of organized crime.

De Rienzo made it a habit to stop in at Frank's Luncheonette—a handful of tables, a counter, a convenient backroom—to talk with old acquaintances. Among them was one Anthony Tavolaris, a burly dark-complected six-footer known to De Rienzo and close associates as Knobby. Knobby and Monkey had never been in business together, but as products of the same East New York neighborhood and with a circle of mutual friends and interests, they made easy conversation. Tavolaris was not totally unknown to law enforcement people. He had one minor complaint against him and he was suspected of working for the gambling enterprises run by a Brooklyn crime family.

While Knobby and Monkey reminisced and discoursed on the affairs of contemporaries, the other actors who would join forces with the East New York pals were also making their entrances in what might be called a $2.7-million drama. Stuart Norman was a businessman. Art Amusement Co. and Stuart Vending were two firms he owned and both of them involved the installation of cigarette machines, juke boxes, and coin-operated pool tables in bars in the New York area. Stuart Norman had between forty and fifty customers who shared the revenue from smokers, pool players, and music lovers in saloons. The devices required a considerable investment; the business was highly competitive; Norman supported a wife and three children in a suburb of Long Island. Unfortunately, his clients often went out of business or the emporiums changed hands so swiftly that Norman was frequently engaged in attempts to liberate his costly machines from padlocked stores. In addition, concessionaires such as Norman traditionally have been forced to serve as kind of a low- or no-interest bank for saloons in return for the privilege of keeping the vending machines on the premises. All things considered, Stuart Norman did not enjoy great financial security in the fall of 1969.

On Fort Hamilton Parkway in Brooklyn was a bar managed by Louis Daniels, who was negotiating to buy the place from the owner. The manager, however, was short of cash. He approached Stuart Norman, who agreed to advance $2,000 to Daniels, who not only assured Norman that he would retain the vending machines but inquired whether the concessionaire knew of a way to sell securities. Stuart Norman answered no.

During the course of his rounds, however, Stuart Norman also met with a chunky man in his forties named Sidney Feldstein. He too had hopes of buying a bar, in fact he had his eye on a shuttered saloon called John's Bar, which happened to be adjacent to Frank's Luncheonette where Knobby and Monkey passed the time of day over coffee. Stuart Norman also had an interest in John's Bar. When the previous tenant abandoned the saloon the landlord had locked up the place and one of Stuart Norman's coin-operated pool tables was thus a captive in John's Bar.

Like Lou Daniels, Sid Feldstein also was short of funds; he too touched Stuart Norman for a $2,000 loan. Prospects for repayment from Feldstein appeared dubious; and as a way of reimbursing Norman, Feldstein began helping the businessman on his routes for collections and service of the machines. As they drove through Brooklyn, Sidney Feldstein asked, "Do you know where I could get a good shot at making some money?" The question brought to Norman's mind another question, the one from Louis Daniels on a way to sell some securities.

At Feldstein's urging, and with a growing acceptance of

the possibility himself, Norman steered for the bar on Fort Hamilton Parkway. The manager was not on duty, but he lived nearby. In Daniels' apartment, Norman introduced Feldstein as a fellow with the proper connections. Daniels responded that he would find out whether the items were still available. While his two visitors waited, he made a telephone call and then informed Feldstein and Norman that the securities consisted of Treasury bills, about $3,000,000 worth, he said.

The conferees agreed to meet subsequently with another principal. At the appointed time, Stuart Norman and Sidney Feldstein traveled to Lou Daniels' place where they were introduced to a muscular six-foot, 170-pounder. He had black hair, a goatee, and a pair of hard eyes and went by the name of Vincent Poerio. Apparently satisfied all around with the looks of the participants, Vinnie Poerio set up a meet in a "Spanish" bar.

Meanwhile, back at Frank's Luncheonette, the casual conversations between Knobby and Monkey took a more purposeful direction, enhanced probably by Joe De Rienzo's tendency to expand the importance of his connections. On February 28, 1970, De Rienzo showed up as usual around ten in the morning. "He [Tavolaris] took me over to one side and he asked me if I knew anybody or if I could get rid of some Treasury bills."

"I asked him how much was involved. He told me three million. I told him I knew a guy named Murray in Cedarhurst who I'd done business with who might be interested." Actually De Rienzo had heard vaguely of a fence who went by the name of Murray but had never met him.

It was agreed that Monkey De Rienzo could check with his man and let Knobby Tavolaris know the possibilities. A day later, De Rienzo informed Tavolaris that Murray would pay 11 or 12 points. The news delighted Knobby for another fence had offered a mere 8 points. The difference between the 8 and the 11 or 12 could be split between the two men. Naturally, the dealer would want to see a sample of the goods but Tavolaris boasted that if the thing went through he could lay his hands on $10,000,000 more in similar pieces.

In his 1970 dark-green Oldsmobile, Knobby drove De Rienzo to a house in the Howard Beach neighborhood of Brooklyn. De Rienzo waited outside while his companion entered the building. Inside Sidney Feldstein's apartment were Feldstein and Stuart Norman. The latter had just come from a meeting in the Spanish bar with Vincent Poerio and using separate cars they had driven to Feldstein's address. There, in the street, Poerio handed Stuart Norman a newspaper. In it was a $100,000 Treasury bill. Norman carried the newspaper and its contents into the apartment and spent some time talking with Sidney Feldstein. After Knobby Tavolaris appeared, Norman went into the living room, leaving the $100,000 note on the dining room table as the centerpiece for a chat between the host and Tavolaris.

Outside in the automobile, De Rienzo became slightly restless while waiting for Knobby; he left the car and walked up to the house, where he read the name Feldstein on the door. When Knobby came out of the house, he gave the $100,000 note to his chum from the good old days. They motored back to another bar where De Rienzo retrieved his car and they separated. Around midnight, De Rienzo showed up at the home of Tavolaris in the Ozone Park section of Queens, carrying the glad news that the piece would fetch 12 points.

The fact of the matter was that De Rienzo never approached any potential buyer for the securities. As a small timer with less and less entree into organized crime he had no contacts. Instead of showing the $100,000 bill to a Murray or his equivalent, De Rienzo carried it home, as he explained later in court, flashed it before his astonished brother-in-law and then squirreled it away in his apartment. The relatives in the family asked whether it was genuine and from whom De Rienzo had obtained the certificate. He fobbed them off with the story that he was only holding the bill in safekeeping for a friend.

On Monday, March 3, 1970, De Rienzo decided that he had perhaps gotten into waters that were not only well over his head but that there might even be a deadly undertow. He telephoned the Federal Bureau of Investigation offices in New York City. The agent who took the call, however, decided that what was involved was a matter of counterfeiting.

At 6 P.M. on Monday, De Rienzo rendezvoused with Secret Service Agent Richard A. Jagen in a drugstore across the street from the offices of the Secret Service in lower Manhattan. Later, in the chambers of the Treasury men, De Rienzo related his story and showed bill 1017965A, a $100,000 note.

Operating on the theory that this was a large-scale counterfeit caper (the Secret Service did not check any lists of stolen bills), the Secret Service made arrangements to stake out the meeting places where De Rienzo would join the conspirators. The informant was equipped with a raincoat; when he had seen the bills he was to remove his coat, fold it over his arms and the agents would rush in for the arrest.

In light of his background, it's reasonable to wonder about De Rienzo's conversion to honesty. "I don't know why I did it," he said later. "I suddenly got religion and I figure if I helped them [the feds] they would help me start a new life." The foundation for a "new life" would be two or three points that De Rienzo expected Morgan Guaranty to pay as a reward. De Rienzo was streetwise enough to know that as much as five points will be paid for recovery of outstanding securities. Virtue carries more than its own reward.

The whole business of rewards and buybacks is a subject of debate among law enforcement agencies. "We had a rigid code not to buy back anything," said Joe Leahy of the New York forces. "The FBI creates a market for things, they're stolen because it's known the FBI will buy back," insisted Leahy. "Of course they demand that any buyback must be accompanied by an arrest. But the same as in gambling, you get accommodation arrests. They get some standup guy to do a little time for the big guys. Everybody knows we have a stiff stuck with the stuff on him." Leahy's alliteration aside, one aspect that sets the FBI apart from local police is that the feds appear to have access to buyback money while the New York City cops do not. Buyback money is a powerful corruption aphrodisiac. However, in truth, the FBI only has money to pay informants, sums ordinarily in the nature of $200. Buyback money comes from the victims—the banks, brokerage houses, and insurance companies.

At Frank's Luncheonette on the morning of March 4, however, Knobby reported to De Rienzo that the source had failed to produce the rest of the bills. De Rienzo dutifully went to a gas station and using a telephone booth pretended to call his people to report the postponement of the transaction. The agents and the quarry all hung around the area awaiting consummation of the deal. At two in the afternoon, Knobby left the place agreeing he'd return with the merchandise. But he came back empty-handed.

"My buyer is not going to stand still for this," threatened double agent De Rienzo. "He's going to kill the whole deal." Tavolaris promised to have the stuff the next morning. Everyone drove off; the agents in fact were under the impression that something might be pulled off at Kennedy Airport and they watched the TWA terminal for several hours but saw nothing.

At 6 P.M., De Rienzo met with Tavolaris in Tom's Bar in East New York. Knobby had a companion, Stuart Norman, whom De Rienzo had never met before. "This guy's got the bills," said Tavolaris. "Let's go to your buyer's house." De Rienzo agreed to try for a meeting. But when he discreetly telephoned the Secret Service from another gas station booth he found that since it was after 6 P.M. there was no agent on duty and no one to handle his situation. He called his wife to make protracted conversation and then returned to Tom's Bar. In the interval, he concocted a tale that the dealer was busy entertaining house guests and did not have the proper amount of cash on hand for such short notice. If, however, the T bills could be delivered at noon the following day, the deal could be consummated.

At 7:30 A.M. Anthony Tavolaris telephoned his friend Monkey and instructed him to appear at Frank's by 9:30. An increasingly nervous De Rienzo then tried to reach the Secret Service. But it was too early for anyone to have reported for work. He was able to leave a message and ten or fifteen minutes later the agents returned the call and agreed to the setup. De Rienzo, however, was so strung out that he left his home without the raincoat designed to serve as a signal.

Around the same time, Stuart Norman, received the package of Treasury bills from Vincent Poerio. When Norman walked into the luncheonette, De Rienzo asked to see the material. Frank's Luncheonette offered very little privacy for such confidential business dealings but the trio retired to a small storage room in the back. While Tavolaris played lookout, De Rienzo and Norman retired into a closet that housed the toilet. Stuart Norman unbuttoned his shirt and removed the package with the securities from its hiding place against his chest. De Rienzo glanced at the Treasury bills long enough to see several pieces with long strings of zeros preceded by the number one. In court, De Rienzo reported that Norman replaced the manila envelope against his body and buttoned his shirt.

With Monkey apparently satisfied, the trio headed out the door of the luncheonette. They approached the car single file. Tavolaris led the way to his car where he would unlock the door. Stuart Norman was in the middle and De Rienzo brought up the rear. Unfortunately, the double agent had no raincoat to doff and drape over his arm for a signal. On the brisk March day he had to hope that removal of his sport jacket would be recognized by agents, hopefully lurking nearby.

Secret Service man Jagen was no longer convinced that this was a counterfeit operation and so the mixed bag of law enforcement also included FBI personnel. When De Rienzo removed his jacket, the agents accepted that as their signal and to the immediate chagrin of Tavolaris and Norman, they swooped down upon the men from several directions and made the arrest. From Norman the agents retrieved $2.7 million of Morgan Guaranty's T bills. Neither of the other two men had any incriminating material on them. To protect the star witness, all three individuals went through the same booking procedure and the government made no sign that any of the trio was less culpable than the others. Satisfied that the T bills were genuine, the Secret Service withdrew from the case. It was FBI material now.

At this point the government's case was only against Tavolaris and Norman. De Rienzo had had no contact with Vinnie Poerio or Lou Daniels. He could point out the house in Howard Beach where Tavolaris had driven him and where he had seen the name Feldstein on the mailbox but that hardly was enough evidence to indict Feldstein.

For the next four months De Rienzo occupied himself mainly with daily attendance at Aqueduct race track. Occasionally at Frank's he saw his pal Knobby, out on bail, for it would have been indiscreet for De Rienzo to change his habits abruptly. And conceivably, Tavolaris in the course of conversation, might drop added information on the original source of the T bills. Knobby, however, supplied no details except to confidently boast, "It's no sweat. Those bills weren't found on us."

As time passed, however, Tavolaris began to have some second thoughts about what had occurred. Possibly he began to wonder how his friend who had no visible means of support managed to play the horses regularly. In fact, Tavolaris actually borrowed $1,000 from De Rienzo, which, instead of making him grateful for a friend in need may have heightened his suspicions. Actually, De Rienzo was living on some $10,000 paid out by Morgan Guaranty as part of its reward for the recovery of the stolen paper.

At one meeting in late spring subsequent to the arrest, Knobby approached Monkey with a chilling idea. "He asked me to set up a meeting with a certain person," remembered De Rienzo on the witness stand, "and I says this person would be very hard to get to." Tavolaris grew angry and he insisted, "You could do it. Somebody ratted us out and I want to find out who it is."

The "certain person" was Tommy Eboli [called Tommy Ryan by De Rienzo], now in his short-lived ascendency to take over the Genovese family business. Like the FBI, organized crime also works through informers; the chief difference between the two networks of information is that one is on the fringe or inside organized crime and the other is on the fringe of law enforcement or part of the police-judicial operation. Under the circumstances Tavolaris obviously thought a don like Eboli, if so inclined, could find out who ratted on the deal. Actually,

De Rienzo's ties to Eboli had been part of the con he fed Tavolaris during their many coffee chats, but said De Rienzo, "It wasn't true that I was still connected with Tommy Ryan. At most I worked for people who worked for Ryan in 1964 but that was all over." De Rienzo did seek out an alleged soldier who refused to carry word to Eboli. Monkey reached his old boss Agro, but he too would not intercede.

One day at the race track, while loitering near the $50 windows, which he claimed were too rich for his wallet, De Rienzo was accosted by Tavolaris who led him to the cafeteria on the third deck of the track. Tavolaris introduced him to "Jimmy," a middle-aged well-dressed man with "salt-and-pepper hair," as De Rienzo described him. Tavolaris strolled off a few feet to permit a confidential conversation between De Rienzo and Jimmy. "A lot of people lost a lot of money on those T notes," Jimmy advised Monkey, who could only make noises of commiseration. For several minutes Jimmy impressed his companion with the unhappiness of investors in the T bills and hinted that anyone responsible for their loss to the authorities would suffer unpleasant consequences.

The pressure upon De Rienzo mounted. On July 4, 1970, Tavolaris asked his old friend to join him at a diner. Joe De Rienzo was directed to enter a nearby automobile. He was unable to see the face of another man in the car, only the fellow's eyes. They made a great impression upon the increasingly frightened De Rienzo. "The eyes, the eyes, I could never forget them, penetrating, penetrating." There was a brief colloquy about the identity of the informer. De Rienzo muttered some threats of his own to convince the stranger of his own embarrassment. The newcomer then offered some words equally scary as his hard eyes. "We have thirty guys waiting to see who ratted us out. That goes without saying. When that guy gets on the stand, then the guy gets caught. We will handle it." In the event that De Rienzo had failed to perceive the message, Tavolaris then backed him up against a tree after the chief prosecution witness left the stranger's car. "When I find the guy, I'm going to bury him." To emphasize the point, Knobby dug the toe of his well-shod foot into the ground.

Still, De Rienzo hung around Brooklyn, made his visits to the track. But in mid-July he received a peremptory summons from Tavolaris to meet at the luncheonette again. "No ifs, ands, or buts, you better be there." To De Rienzo it was a cue for a disappearing act and the U.S. Attorney's office agreed. Under the witness protection program of the Justice Department, an individual vital to the prosecution of a case and whose well-being is threatened—before, during, or after trial—can be reincarnated, given a new identity when his services are completed. The witness is supposed to be relocated and bureaucratically reborn, as a new person is created out of officially faked Social Security, military, and school records. On paper, it seems like a simple procedure, but it's highly fallible. Gerald Martin Zelmanowitz, a man who spent most of his adult life in white-collar crime, stock swindles, deals in stolen securities, bribery, and tax fraud fell into government hands finally and turned on his associates in organized crime. Zelmanowitz thought he was fully protected through the witness protection program that relocated him in San Francisco under a new name. He entered legitimate business there, achieved some reputation as a philanthropic and civic-minded fellow and then became embroiled in a complex battle for control of a company he headed. The opposition hired private detectives to discover anything damaging in Zelmanowitz's background, and the cover allegedly provided him was not even paper thin. Nobody had bothered to manufacture the appropriate documents that would have given Zelmanowitz a foundation for his new identity.

Whatever the other failures in the program, Joe De Rienzo was successfully relocated in Baltimore with a new name and a job driving a milk truck. His family remained in Brooklyn. He stayed in Baltimore out of sight until the 1972 trial of Anthony Tavolaris and Stuart Norman. The defendants and all of the losers on the T-bill scheme of course now knew who the informant was; the prosecution is obligated to make known to the defense who its witnesses will be well before the trial begins.

The defense attacked the credibility of Joe De Rienzo. Introduced in evidence were notes supposedly written by him to Tavolaris demanding $500. The prosecution countered that these were simply requests for repayment of the $1,000 loan made to Tavolaris; and Knobby actually did give De Rienzo the $1,000 in two payments. There was also a homemade tape recording of a telephone call allegedly from Monkey. A voice identified by Tavolaris as that of De Rienzo said, "Give me some money. I'll get out of town." On the tape Tavolaris responded, "But you know I'm innocent." The other person said, "I know you're innocent, but I need money to get out of town. And you will never hear from me again." Tavolaris claimed that the recording had been done by his son, who hooked up a homemade system when De Rienzo called. De Rienzo, while admitting that some of the voice on the tape may have sounded like his, denied that he ever made any such call. De Rienzo's credibility suffered somewhat with his confession that even after the arrest outside of Frank's Luncheonette he had continued to engage in larcenous schemes. He tried to defraud a bank with a falsified loan application and there was some suggestion that the government intervened to ensure leniency. De Rienzo made complete restitution, but the jury might easily have con-

cluded that De Rienzo was repaying a favor to the government with his testimony.

When Anthony Tavolaris took the witness stand in his
own defense, he said he was in the company of Stuart Norman on the day of the arrest just to be a good guy. With
Norman anxious to remove the pool table from the adjoin-
ing bar, Tavolaris claimed that he had been asked by the
landlord to hold the key and wait for Norman at Frank's.
He insisted he knew nothing of the Treasury bills until
after he was arrested. He denied any threats to De Rienzo.

Sidney Feldstein had been subpoenaed to appear at the
trial which was held in Westbury, Long Island. He failed
to show up on the appointed day however. When a witness
for the prosecution does not appear there is an implication,
sometimes it's even explicitly stated by the judge, that the
witness has turned out to be damaging to the prosecution
rather than helpful. Feldstein missed his day in court,
however, not because the U.S. Attorneys felt he would be
injurious to the prosecution. Instead his excuse was he had
misread his subpoena and gone to the courthouse in
Brooklyn instead of to Westbury. The government attorneys had assumed Feldstein would be a friendly witness
because he was not indicted. They regarded his absence at
Westbury as a hostile act. Later he would confirm this appraisal.

Although Stuart Norman copped a guilty plea, he was
not a very effective witness. He offered a minimum of information and that rather late in the game. The jury
weighed the testimony of both sides, advised the judge
that it was a standoff between those who believed Joe De
Rienzo and those who believed Anthony Tavolaris. There
was no alternative but to declare a mistrial for Knobby.
Stuart Norman pleaded guilty, but the government described him in the presentation report as minimally cooperative. The judge gave him a five-year term.

A U.S. Attorney present in the court at the time recalls the scene at the sentencing. "Norman's wife had broken a foot or leg. She was on crutches. When the judge said five years, she began to scream, she fell on the floor and grabbed at Norman's pants legs."

There was one other loser as a result of the trial: Special Agent Andy Watson. Two years of investigation under Watson had not unveiled The Person. The trial of Tavolaris was the third prosecution in which the defendants had not been found guilty and in which it seemed that the evidence produced by the FBI was insufficient to convict. As the agent in command of the Morgan case, Watson, under Bureau rules, was required to file a report on every individual within five days of the arrest. With so many individuals picked up, and no help from his superiors, Watson fell far behind in his paper work. As much for administrative failures as investigative fluffs, Watson was punished by his superiors with a thirty-day suspension and transferred to Detroit.

The stiff sentence meted out to Stuart Norman had its desired effect. He turned into a much more cooperative fellow. Norman now told the government much more about the transaction, bringing in the names of Lou Daniels and Vincent Poerio. A fingerprint expert from Washington managed to find Lou Daniels' mark upon several of the T bills. And for the first time, the character of Vincent Poerio entered the judicial proceedings. As the government learned in its action against Harold Goerlich, testimony of an accomplice to a crime, which was Norman's role, is a frail reed. Physical evidence or testimony by another person to buttress the story is highly desirable. Against Daniels, the latent fingerprints sufficed. For Poerio, the government went back to Joe De Rienzo. While the informer had never actually been able to see Poerio's face, the impression of the penetrating eyes remained clearly engraved upon De Rienzo's memory. Supposedly, he identified Poerio six times from collections of mug shots placed before him by U.S. Attorneys.

The second trial, for the attempt to pass stolen Treasury bills with Joe De Rienzo as a middleman, began November 4, 1974, in Brooklyn. Anthony Tavolaris—joined by Vincent Poerio, already serving time in Atlanta for trafficking in narcotics, and Louis Daniels—stood before the bar on the charge that they did conspire "to receive, possess, cancel, store, sell, and dispose of U.S. Treasury bills, particularly $100,000 Treasury bill serial #1017965A but not limited to that bill."

The case against Knobby was basically the same as on his first go-around, although the added details supplied by Stuart Norman etched a clearer picture of Tavolaris's role. His defense relied again upon the character of the two men who identified him as a participant in the plot. Gus Newman, counsel for Tavolaris, in his opening statement suggested there was a lack of evidence in face of the requirement to establish beyond reasonable doubt the guilt of the accused. Newman suggested to the jury that it view the prosecution witness from an interesting standard: "Is he the kind of guy I'd buy a used car from?" Gus Newman then ripped into De Rienzo. "I will establish to your satisfaction that he's a burglar, that he broke into a store at night to steal [this was an offense committed twenty-one years ago]. He was a shylock; he lent money to people at exorbitant rates of interest and that in addition to violating the law, it was standard operating procedure for [De Rienzo] to do his friends in."

The defense for Poerio pointed out that the accused was not even arrested until April of 1974, more than three years after the attempt to dispose of the bills. And in the course of the trial, when Joe De Rienzo identified Poerio as the man who obliquely threatened him in the car outside of the diner and implicated himself in the transaction, the defendant burst out, "He is a liar, he never met me in my life. He's a liar." Judge Thomas Platt advised Poerio to speak through his attorney. Poerio, perhaps in deference to prison rules, no longer sported a goatee. He also wore spectacles, which hid the so-called penetrating eyes, and it was noted that De Rienzo never remarked upon a clearly visible scar on Poerio's cheek.

Defense counselors for both Poerio and Lou Daniels attacked the credibility of Stuart Norman on the grounds that he had served only two years of his five-year term and that his testimony was an unwritten condition for his probation. The U.S. Attorney and the witness both denied any such quid pro quo.

The jury heard the famous home recording that alleged to be De Rienzo's try to blackmail Tavolaris. The government witness again denied that the voice belonged to him. And three notes, supposedly written by De Rienzo that demanded money, also were introduced. De Rienzo accepted responsibility for only one of these. He reiterated that it merely represented a request for payment on the loan to Knobby.

Sidney Feldstein appeared as a defense witness, insisting that he actually had never met Vinny Poerio, a flat contradiction of the words from Stuart Norman. In rebuttal, the prosecution produced an FBI agent who had questioned Feldstein after Stuart Norman told all, and in that interrogation Feldstein had admitted to being present when Poerio passed the T bill in a newspaper to Norman. Furthermore, Judge Platt was outraged over Feldstein's account of how he erred on the location of the first trial and became a no-show.

Naturally De Rienzo's criminal record was emphasized to the jury. Since the first trial, he had become enmeshed in another illegal escapade, a better than $900 swindle of a cousin. Caught, he again made restitution and escaped with further probation.

The jury returned a verdict of guilty against all three men. Anthony Tavolaris received a pair of five-year concurrent terms. Vinny Poerio had two concurrent five-year terms tacked onto those he faced for a dope violation charge. Lou Daniels caught a pair of three-year concurrent terms.

Stuart Norman continued to try to piece together his life as a businessman. There was some thought given to a prosecution of Sidney Feldstein for perjury in view of his testimony. Under oath he said he never met Poerio although the FBI investigator's notes clearly indicated that Feldstein had admitted to this incident. Feldstein had all along skated at the narrow edge of indictment. "He was really peripheral to the case," said Assistant U.S. Attorney James Dougherty, who eventually prosecuted the second trial. "I came into the case late. Until then, there was always the hope that Feldstein would be a cooperative witness and it was felt that holding the possibility of an indictment over his head would make the difference. After I started on the case I told him to come in and see me. He said he'd talk to his lawyer and agreed to come in. But he never showed up for the appointment. By then it was getting late to go for a superseding indictment that would include Feldstein in the case."

During the trial, Joe De Rienzo lived in a hotel under the guard of U.S. marshals. He saw his wife and children intermittently. After the jury declared the three accused men guilty, the marshals took De Rienzo to the airport where he bought a ticket for some place unknown to even Jim Dougherty. This was the second time the witness protection program had given De Rienzo a new identity, but again he was to destroy his anonymous character by the commission of a crime. De Rienzo insisted that the niggardly behavior of the government forced him into his petty swindles. "If they'd keep their promises and given me two or three points of what was recovered [or a reward of over $50,000], I could have gone away with my family and made a life for myself." The actual bounty paid to De Rienzo added up to roughly $25,000.

There's not much question that the star witness was in danger. After he exposed his first new life, Monkey returned to Brooklyn. Sneaking visits to his family, he never slept in the same place two nights in a row. But one February night in 1973 about 2 A.M., De Rienzo was accosted on a Brooklyn street. "Get in that green Buick," ordered a tall man in a raincoat, who demonstrated his authority with a glimpse of a pistol.

De Rienzo sat in the back with the raincoat-clad man, while another hood drove the Buick. "Empty your pockets, everything in this paper bag," said the tall man. The hit man took De Rienzo's wallet, even searched him for a religious medal or identification tag.

"I'm dead, they're going to bury me," concluded De Rienzo.

The Buick rolled into the borough of Queens. The driver, as De Rienzo noticed, observed all full stops and traffic lights; it would be inopportune to be halted for a traffic violation. The Buick stopped for a signal in the Ridgewood section of Queens, just across from a big gas station that remained open all night. De Rienzo hit the door handle with his elbow; mercifully the doors were not locked. He rolled out of the car and bounced on the pavement smacking his head. On his feet, De Rienzo raced into the gas station. The Buick followed.

"Call the cops, they're trying to kill me," the bloody-faced De Rienzo yelled at the attendants. The hunted man scrambled toward the back of the service station to hide. At that moment another car innocently in search of gas pulled up at one of the pumps. The green Buick gave up the chase and drove off.

Since the second trial De Rienzo has gone partially underground. He has not sought another reincarnation from the Justice Department. He simply lives on the run, with a little help from the New York State police, who have interceded to help De Rienzo create another new identity.

XI

The Double Agent

The informer ploy appears in many guises. In some cases the source, like Monkey De Rienzo, inevitably surfaces. In other incidents, the informer retains anonymity while reaping rewards.

Around noon on March 10, 1970, Samuel Schwartz, a 55-year-old white man, still trim and dapper at five-feet-eight and 140 pounds, met two other men in the lobby of the Commodore Hotel, Manhattan. One of the two, Fred Sands, was a fairly recent acquaintance of Samuel Schwartz and the third party, Tony Rose, was a total stranger. Fred Sands made the introductions and the trio took a table in the bar of the Commodore for a business discussion.

Tony Rose, explained Fred Sands to Schwartz, was most anxious to procure stolen securities. He was prepared in fact to spend as much as $3,000,000 on such pieces if they were available. Schwartz bragged that he could locate as much as $6,000,000 worth of the stuff. If Tony was interested Schwartz could supply Treasury bills for 8 points. They haggled over price, until they settled on 5.5 points as the price. However, Schwartz cautioned that he faced "the age-old problem. I don't know you personally, and I don't have any reference for you except for Fred's. And him I only know for six weeks. He's been awfully slow about getting in touch once I brought up the subject."

Tony Rose said, "I'm from Montreal, and I represent the old man." Sam Schwartz still had his doubts, however. He asked to see some tangible evidence of Tony Rose's good faith. That was a perfectly reasonable request to Rose. He and Samuel Schwartz walked across the street to a branch of the Bowery Savings Bank. Tony Rose signed himself into the vault premises as Harold Michaels, holder of box 24. The custodian, with Rose accompanying him, removed box 24 from the vault to a small room. In the privacy of that chamber, Tony Rose opened the box and showed Sam Schwartz $90,000 in currency. That appeared to convince the doubtful Schwartz that Rose had come to deal seriously.

Back at the Commodore, Schwartz informed the pair that the T bills had a number of weeks to maturity date. There were several pieces worth a million each plus various $100,000 and $50,000 items. Samuel Schwartz excused himself to make a telephone call. When he returned he said, "My people want to sell one or two pieces at a time until they total $1,000,000."

"That's not acceptable," said Rose. "We want at least $1,000,000 at a time." Samuel Schwartz excused himself once more and after his second telephone call announced there would be a $500,000, four $100,000s, and a $50,000 available.

The proposal was accepted. The parties agreed to reconvene that evening at the Commodore.

Shortly before 7 P.M. they assembled and Samuel Schwartz apologized. "I can only get a $500,000 at this time." Tony Rose voiced unhappiness with the failure to meet the contractual specifications. "I'll see if I can work it out," promised Schwartz. "My people have come in from Brooklyn to the Mott Street area [a neighborhood where New York's Chinatown abuts an old Italo-American section]. I'll have to take a trip and see if I can get the stuff."

"Go ahead," instructed Tony Rose. But first, Samuel Schwartz felt it necessary to call his principal. He used a Commodore Hotel telephone booth, while Tony Rose waited next to the booth. Rose heard Schwartz address his contact as Louis several times, and then Schwartz stepped out of the booth and beckoned to Rose. "Louis wants to talk to you."

The voice on the other end of the line complained to Rose, "What do you think you're buying here, Cracker Jacks?"

"What do you think we're paying for these things with, Cracker Jacks?" retorted Tony Rose. The two men argued over the telephone about the pieces that had been agreed upon with Schwartz. Finally, the call was terminated with no resolution. Schwartz departed, promising to call Fred when everything was in order. But when no word came from Schwartz, Fred called him at his home. Schwartz confessed that his people were still nervous about Tony Rose's credentials and feared a setup.

Tony Rose got on the phone and flatly informed Schwartz, "I'm going back to the old man in Canada, unless you people want to deal." On March 11, Fred again contacted Schwartz who still expressed anxiety about the buyers. Schwartz suggested that Fred telephone every half hour and as soon as Schwartz received any word from his people he'd advise the others. Perhaps five calls later, Schwartz announced that he would have $1,000,000 in Treasury bills at the Commodore at five that afternoon.

At 5:10 P.M. the three met in the bar. It was agreed that Sam would show the securities to Fred (whom he obviously trusted more than Tony Rose) in the lobby of the hotel while Tony Rose was to go to his room, 2144, of the Commodore. If Fred Sands found the pieces satisfactory, he would use a house phone to notify Tony Rose. The exchange of cash for the stolen bills would then take place.

Sam Schwartz ducked out a side entrance of the hotel as Sands headed for the lobby and Rose for the elevator to take him to the twenty-first floor. In due time, Sands called on the house phone to Rose and said they were coming up. In the privacy of room 2144, Tony Rose and Fred Sands looked upon the four bills, all of which appeared to be in order. Tony Rose excused himself for a moment and dialed room 2146. In a low voice he read off the serial number for the $500,000 bill. A few minutes later, three agents of the FBI burst into room 2144 and arrested all three men.

Meanwhile, in the upper lobby of the Commodore, other FBI agents had their eyes on a shapely woman, Sam Schwartz's wife, Sonia. Schwartz had been observed doubling back to the Commodore where she passed him some papers. Almost thirty years younger than her husband, Sonia Schwartz, when grabbed by the FBI agents, protested that she knew nothing about the stolen securities. She was at the Commodore to meet Samuel who had promised to take her out to dinner.

Sam Schwartz had done a long stretch in a federal penitentiary for dealing in counterfeit money. The last pride he seemed to have in life was Sonia Schwartz. "Down at the FBI office," said an agent who was in on the arrest, "Schwartz decided to cop out, if we would make a deal to free his wife. 'Cut her loose and I'll give you my connec-

tion.' It's now nine or ten o'clock at night. We really don't
have an iron-clad with his wife. She was just there, may
not have known the stuff was stolen. The U.S. Attorney finally agrees that we can make the deal.

"Schwartz says that his connection is Louis Pergola and
that Pergola has a lot more of the Treasury bills. We know
Pergola as a major supplier of stolen securities and very
much in organized crime [the Senate Subcommittee hearings also named Pergola as a trafficker in stolen securities].

"He calls Pergola and makes a meet," remembers the
agent. "It was for some place with a fancy French-like
name but it was really a luncheonette. We cut Sam's wife
loose and stake out this place but Pergola never shows up.
We must have waited until midnight or one in the morning
but there's no Louis Pergola. We went over to a restaurant
in the Coney Island neighborhood, a place owned by a
mob guy Paddy Marcello who's known to us. We spot
Louie's car there and he finally comes staggering out to
the street around 4 A.M. with some chippie on his arm. We
grabbed him but he was absolutely clean. We made a big
mistake when we cut Schwartz's wife loose. She probably
called Pergola, and I would guess that Schwartz told her
to. When you're tied up with the wise guys, you don't turn
'em in."

Fred Sands was an FBI informant and Tony Rose an undercover agent of the FBI. The official reports of the FBI
used by members of the Strike Force Against Organized
Crime spell out the parts played by Sands and Rose, but
that is only part of the story. "When the FBI arrests five
guys for dealing in stolen securities," says Joe Leahy, for-
merly with the New York Bond and Forgery Squad, "one
of them goes to jail and the other four are out on the street
as informants for the FBI." An FBI agent who spent ten
years in the Bureau's organized crime section and did undercover work confirms Leahy, in principle if not in pro-

portions. "One out of every two people dealing in stolen securities is also an informant. What you have to watch out for is that the sources often don't tell the whole story. They often operate on a one for the FBI and two for me basis. If they throw enough buddies to the Bureau they hope to get enough room to work for themselves on occasion."

It was one of these informants, Fred Sands, who tipped off a Bureau agent that Samuel Schwartz was negotiating stolen Treasury bills. And it was Fred Sands that arranged for Tony Rose's introduction to Schwartz and some guarantee of his trustworthiness. For the services rendered in the case of Sam Schwartz, with the subsequent recovery of close to $1,000,000 of face value Treasury bills, the informant's reward should have been about $50,000, or the equivalent of five points, roughly the same amount that Schwartz wanted. Under these circumstances it's not difficult to see why hustlers would as lief deal with the FBI as with peddlers of stolen securities. The profit is the same, the risks are not much greater if one is careful.

Morgan Guaranty footed the bill for the reward to Fred Sands. It also provided the front money, the $90,000 in currency that Tony Rose showed to Samuel Schwartz as evidence of good faith.

The arrest of Sam Schwartz brought the FBI tantalizingly close to apprehension of someone inside organized crime. While Samuel Schwartz failed to turn over one of the wise guys, he was cooperative enough for the government to pick up another $350,000 in Morgan pieces.

Although the feds had no case against Sonia Schwartz, her husband faced a cheerless prospect of prolonged confinement. His well-blotted escutcheon would be a red flag to a hanging judge. Schwartz bought the best deal he could make; he agreed to enlighten agents on the movement of additional pieces from the Morgan Guaranty theft.

Schwartz's fumble into the hands of agent Tony Rose happened to be his second encounter with hot paper from the World Series caper. More than a month before his financial ship sank in the Commodore Hotel, Schwartz had been contacted for a meet with Louis Pergola. "The stuff from the Morgan Guaranty Trust you know about," said Pergola. "There's $10,000,000 available. Can you move some of it?"

Schwartz allowed as to some potential leads and set off to find takers. Through a bookmaker named Charlie Fine, Schwartz entered into negotiations with a fellow described in FBI reports as Harry LNU (last name unknown). The site for the conference was a table at the Mish Mosh Bar in Brooklyn. But Harry LNU proved to be as insubstantial as his surname. Schwartz went searching for another customer.

Charlie Fine contributed another name, Ray Arthur, a youngish man of no visible means who shared a room at the Dryden East Hotel in New York with an attractive young woman. Schwartz, Fine, and Arthur bargained for a time until Arthur agreed to take $350,000 worth of Morgan's T bills. The notes were procured from Louis Pergola. Schwartz, Fine, and Arthur then drove from the Dryden East to the town of Irvington, New Jersey. The trio did not go directly to the branch office of the First National State of New Jersey Bank where Arthur expected to pass the bills, however. Instead, Arthur called the bank several times from a telephone booth. He was apparently waiting until the head cashier left on his lunch break.

Satisfied at last that the way was clear, Arthur entered the bank. He stayed for some time, according to Schwartz, but emerged at last with a cashier's check for close to $350,000 as a result of pledging the T bills for a loan. On the next day, the three men, with Fine's boss Wally Green, returned to the Irvington bank where Arthur exchanged the cashier's check for hard currency. From this wad he tipped Fine and Green $1,750 each.

Sam Schwartz's tale sent the FBI looking for Ray Arthur and the T bills. The latter were recovered at the bank. Unfortunately, that did not automatically restore to Morgan Guaranty its stolen paper. The New Jersey bank claimed to have accepted the bills in good faith, paid out a lot of cash. Morgan Guaranty began a protracted litigation for the recovery of its T bills.

It was somewhat easier to lay hands on Ray Arthur. At the Dryden East, the FBI learned the hotel's recent guest had moved out, leaving an unpaid bill of $641.20. But the agents discovered a bellhop who admitted he assisted Arthur when he skipped. The bellhop had helped Arthur load his belongings into two Cadillacs which were driven to an elegant new apartment house on Manhattan's upper East Side.

Although Arthur, Fine, and Green were thus arrested through the information of Schwartz, the government found it difficult to prosecute them. The case against the trio remained untried in mid-1975 because of a series of legal machinations.

Samuel Schwartz, who had returned to Pergola for fresh T bills after he witnessed the success enjoyed by Arthur, earned himself a dismissal for his cooperation. Louis Pergola also was awarded a pass. In his case, however, it was with great reluctance. The government had only the word of Samuel Schwartz, a most impeachable witness. And considering Pergola's connections, it is even questionable whether Schwartz would have been willing to testify against him.

XII

Art Lovers,
Coin Collectors,
Card Dealers,
and Simple Cheats

The most disheartening fact gleaned from all of these capers was that the bundle of securities removed from the custody section of Morgan Guaranty was no longer intact. It had split into many pieces and the FBI was condemned to trying to retrieve a bucket of water thrown into the air. The largest single recovery, $2.7 million, had been with the arrest of Norman, Tavolaris, and Poerio through Monkey De Rienzo's tip. A sampling of a number of other recoveries, however, indicates how exceptional this was.

In January, 1970, a Fort Lee, New Jersey men's clothing jobber, Albert Schwartz, brought to the Bankers Trust in Manhattan a $10,000 Treasury bill which he wanted to use to pay off a $1,500 loan. Schwartz spoke briefly with the official and then excused himself because he was double parked and was nervous about a traffic ticket. By the time he had found a safe place for his automobile and returned to the bank, the FBI had already been alerted to the appearance of a stolen Treasury bill. Albert Schwartz was arrested. Originally he insisted the bill was pressed upon him by a lady friend. She vigorously denied any such largesse. He pleaded guilty to possession of the piece and received a year's probation. He was unable to provide any information that would have enabled the investigators to track the movement of the item.

Robert Bialkin was arrested in Athol, Massachusetts, in February, 1970, for a try at passing a pair of $100,000 notes. A well-educated man whose dress and demeanor fitted perfectly into the mold of the law-abiding businessman, Bialkin was at the time an escaped prisoner from the federal penitentiary at Lewisburg. He had a history as a channel for securities obtained by organized crime, much to the dismay of members of his family engaged in the respectable securities market. Bialkin pleaded guilty to some of the charges against him and a compassionate judge sentenced him to five years, suspended, on the proviso that he seek psychiatric help. He was returned to Lewisburg to serve some additional time for his escape and previous crime. These incarcerations were also shortened in favor of therapy.

In July of 1970, well beyond the maturity dates for the Treasury bills, a team of federal agents swooped down upon a car in a shopping center located in suburban Rockville Centre, New York. Inside the automobile, the agents located a pair of Marcel Duchamp originals, *Chocolate Grinder No. 1* and *Portrait of the Artist's Father*. They had disappeared while en route from the Philadelphia Museum of Art to the American Academy of Arts and Letters in New York City. Together the paintings were valued at $95,000. The search of the vehicle produced two $100,000 Morgan Guaranty Treasury bills. Arrested at the scene for possession of the items were Victor Careccia, 34, an unemployed truck driver, Peter John D'Amato, 39, unemployed, and Richard Juliano, 30, described in *The Times* as a life insurance salesman, but known to the cops through four arrests for bookmaking.

The trio had been prepared to make a package sale of both paintings and the U.S. Treasury bills. In D'Amato's wallet, the agents found the business card of a Spring Valley, New York, accountant named Lewis Queen. The auditor when questioned admitted only to knowing D'Amato through a brassy woman, Kate O'Brien. Queen claimed he met with D'Amato and Mrs. O'Brien in a plan to sell a landmark Brooklyn restaurant, Lundys. When the prospective buyers backed out of the deal, Queen admitted to hearing some talk from his associates about using some stolen securities to purchase the place for themselves. However, he of course never thought there was any serious intent by those present actually to sell illegal paper.

Queen and Mrs. O'Brien were not indicted. The three men grabbed in Rockville Centre copped pleas. What is missing from all of the official reports is any mention that they were obviously set up by an informant. Also unrecorded is any statement from the guilty about how they came to possess the Treasury bills. It was one more dead end in the search for The Person.

In the early spring of 1970, José Mendez, an undercover FBI agent, through an intermediary met with a man known as Ralphie. For $10,000, Mendez was supposed to be able to purchase a $100,000 Treasury bill from Ralphie for his boss located in California. As a testament of good faith, Mendez brought Ralphie to a Manhattan bank, and in the fastness of the vault area opened a safe deposit box containing $10,000 packets of cash. Ralphie suggested that Mendez trust him with a packet, but Mendez insisted that he had to receive the T bills before he would fork over any money.

Ralphie drove the intermediary and Mendez around

Brooklyn in a silver Buick Riviera, while other Bureau agents trained cameras. From the photos, Ralphie was later identified as a low-ranking associate of the mob.

About a week later, Mendez arranged a rendezvous with Ralphie at the Hamilton House restaurant in the Sheepshead Bay section of Brooklyn. Mendez importuned Ralphie for a look at the merchandise. Finally, the hoodlum left the restaurant for a brief period. When he returned, he showed Mendez a $100,000 note, numbered 1017038A, a familiar number to those following the Morgan Guaranty case.

Agents, including Mendez, were convinced that Ralphie and his associates held more than the single item displayed for Mendez's benefit. Instead of arranging for a quick arrest, the feds attempted to set up a more ambitious buying program that could lead to the recovery of more than a single piece. Somehow, the criminals became suspicious. Ralphie broke off his negotiations with Mendez and the entire plot collapsed without anything being recovered.

Another failure at least captured the Treasury bill. Two men and a woman were seized on the basis of information and they were found to possess a $100,000 note. But the U.S. Attorney dropped prosecution because the government lacked enough evidence to prove that the trio knew they held a stolen bill.

For the U.S. Attorney, this question of knowledge by an alleged perpetrator blocked a number of prosecutions. Nicholas Lovecchio had the reputation of the family black sheep and was officially known by law enforcement agencies. He negotiated a $10,000 T bill through the offices of a brokerage house, in March of 1970, accepting half of the proceeds in cash, the rest in stock. He supposedly disposed of a $50,000 piece through another firm. FBI agents conducted a thorough study of Lovecchio's background.

They could not shake his story that he received the Treasury bill as security for an old and eventually unpaid debt. For a time, both the frauds office of the Manhattan District Attorney's office and the FBI thought that Lovecchio might be influenced to supply valuable information. Instead, he resolutely denied any intimations of impropriety in his possession of the Treasury bills. The government failed to obtain an indictment against Lovecchio.

In Newark, New Jersey, an individual entered the Garfield Trust Company to seek a large loan. As collateral he proffered $100,000 Treasury bill number 1017013A, which he left with the bankers to examine at their leisure. Having done so, they and various law enforcement agents patiently waited for the return of the would be borrower. He never reappeared. Perhaps as a member or part of one of the other failed attempts to cash the T bills, he realized that the banks posed a poor risk for such transactions. To add to the confusion, the bank received a photocopy of the bill in the mail with no message and no instructions attached. The Garfield Trust Company was a sidebar oddity that lacked even a plausible speculative explanation.

Equally vexatious for those concerned with locking up the malefactors was a scenario that unfolded in Albany, New York. Late in February, 1970, attorney Peter Jefferson deposited a $10,000 T bill and a $1,000 note with the State Bank of Albany for safekeeping to back a loan. The two bills were subsequently sent off to the Federal Reserve in New York City for redemption. To the astonishment of both banker and client in Albany, word came back that the T bills were part of the haul from the custody section at Morgan.

Jefferson explained the complicated circumstances behind his possession of the pair of bills. In January of the same year, a man who called himself George Williamson from Baltimore visited the lawyer to draw up a contract for the purchase of a coin collection valued at $16,000. He put up a $4,000 cashier's check in his name which passed without difficulty. For the balance of the payment Williamson offered three more $4,000 cashier's checks. These proved to be incorrectly drawn, and they bounced back to an embarrassed Peter Jefferson.

Williamson, however, apologized. To remedy the matter he offered a $10,000 T bill and a pair of $1,000 ones. Jefferson, burned once, had the pieces checked and they proved to be good, or at least not on any hot list. When, a month later, Williamson returned to Jefferson's office seeking to float a loan on $11,000 worth of T bills, the attorney did not hesitate to put through the necessary paper work, without pausing to determine if these items also would pass close inspection. Thus, both Jefferson and the State Bank of Albany were victimized by George Williamson.

They were by no means his first marks. Some weeks prior, he had shown up at the home of a Delaware widow impersonating a bank inspector. He invited her cooperation in a plan to trap a swindler who had plotted to embezzle the widow's funds from the bank. To catch the imaginary thief, Williamson inveigled the widow into obtaining a $4,000 cashier's check which he took for safekeeping. That was the down payment on the coin collection.

George Williamson, or whoever he was, vanished from Albany, leaving the FBI only with a description of a man five-foot-eleven, 190 pounds, sandy-haired, in his midforties, and with an appetite for either Seagram's or Canadian Club and water as a pacifier.

Less favored by fortune was George Robert McLaughlin, a habitual trader in hot paper. He frequented a pair of Queens bars, not for the quality of drinks but for the people he might meet. In April, 1970, one of those he contacted was John Lusterino, a.k.a. Johnny Tarzan, a Brooklyn muscle boy with a record that stretched back to 1949.

McLaughlin allowed as how he would not be averse to handling any securities in search of an owner. As a result Lusterino invited McLaughlin to tool along behind his car. They drove several blocks, said McLaughlin, before Johnny Tarzan pulled over to the curb. He walked back to McLaughlin's vehicle and tossed an envelope containing a $1,000,000 T bill through the window of McLaughlin's car.

From Queens, McLaughlin immediately headed for the Port Authority Bus Terminal and parked his car, leaving the T bill locked in the glove compartment. He walked several blocks to rendezvous with a pair of Mexican nationals. The trio then doubled back to the Port Authority building. The foreigners agreed to wait for McLaughlin beside an elevator in the terminal. He hurried to his car, removed the T bill and then joined the two "buyers" beside the elevator. FBI agents made their move, and McLaughlin told his story to members of the U.S. Strike Force.

While he had obviously been set up for the arrest at the Port Authority building by the informant, no one had been present at the time McLaughlin claimed to have received the T bill from John Lusterino. Once again, the best the feds could lay their hands upon was an instrument of organized crime, not the hands that manipulated the tool. And to their bulging files, the agents could add a note that two men who had associations in other illegal ventures, Lusterino and Lazzaro A. San Giovanni, whose name surfaced during the Plumber's caper, both could be vaguely tied to Morgan robbery proceeds.

A Las Vegas card dealer, James Konys, managed to lay his hands upon a $100,000 piece. He entered into an arrangement with a Kansas City lawyer named Henry Tager for the latter to use the bill as collateral against a $30,000 loan. However, an official at the Twin Cities State Bank spotted the pledged note as on the hot list. The dealer copped a guilty plea while Tager fought the case against him. He was found guilty.

A funny thing happened to 53-year-old mortgage broker Herman Simon. As he strolled along Third Avenue in New York City in September of 1971 (nearly two years after the theft) he happened to look into a trash barrel on the corner of Sixty-third Street. Among the rubbish he noticed some very important looking paper; in fact there were five $100,000 pieces dumped there. Simon tucked a pair of them away in his baggage at the Dorset Hotel; slipped three into his jacket. Finders, he discovered, instead of keepers were the losers in the security game. When he displayed one of the three securities in his pocket to a bank official, the FBI was quickly summoned. He received a $1,000 fine, unsupervised probation for a year.

In April of 1971, a good year beyond maturity date, four men were all arrested in Los Angeles and charged with possession of four $100,000 notes. But four years later, the government had still not moved to try them. Three men were also grabbed in Seattle for holding a pair of $100,000 bills. Only one, George De Haven, was found guilty after a trial.

XIII
The Hunt

Recovery of the missing pieces was one-half of the FBI's responsibility. It was the most important part of the job so far as Morgan Guaranty and its insurers were concerned. But the FBI agents had their pride. Feebees had played a small role in recaptures of bills and they were terribly anxious to find both The Person and his direct links into organized crime. In the first two years after the crime, the agents were always ready to sniff a clue and then launch an intensive hunt. Their eagerness made victims of themselves as well as legitimate suspects. And there was no shortage of false scents.

FBI agents in Chicago in 1970 put the clamp on one of the more persistent and more successful stock-fraud artists, Michael Raymond. As Raymond demonstrated during his prolonged testimony before the Senate Subcommittee in subsequent years, his involvement in schemes to transform worthless or stolen paper into gold went beyond the dreams of the most ambitious alchemist.

Mike Raymond grew up in Brooklyn, attended a university in the Midwest and then as a young man during the 1950s became a customer's man for a reputable brokerage firm. He quickly discovered a new métier, boiler room operations. His earliest specialty lay in uranium speculations in which the stock companies formed to mine the new wonder mineral struck gold among investors whose cash was exceeded by both greed and stupidity. Raymond and others in the game took their "box," or list, of customers away from the legitimate brokerage firms and exploited it in the boiler room operations. "A customer's man could control portfolios running into millions of dollars," said Raymond, "and if he switched only 10 percent of a million-dollar portfolio or 20 percent, it involved $2,000,000 or $3,000,000 in churning." Raymond estimated that cash payoffs to an operator such as himself amounted to 20 percent, or $200,000, if he churned $1,000,000 in what were eventually worthless uranium mines.

By the mid-1950s Raymond was already an experienced bucket shop performer and associating with such distinguished defrauders as Peter Crosby and Alexander Guterma. But the dazzling act of balancing seductive prospectuses and visions of beautiful capital gains for suckers suddenly faced an audience of gimlet-eyed government attorneys. Raymond went looking for a new act to distract this audience and he found it in the links between organized crime (embodied by the Genovese family) and well-connected politicians like Nat Voloshen, who had ties with then Speaker of the House John McCormack's aide, Dr. Martin Zweig, and New York State Supreme Court judge, Mitchell D. Schweitzer.

Mike Raymond did minimal prison time for his sins. But his career from then on was a series of intricate turns—government informer, dealer in stolen securities for the mob, and mastermind of illegal schemes. At any given moment in his history it would be difficult to determine which role Raymond really was starring in. Often it was a combination. An FBI agent familiar with Raymond described the act from a government seat: "He'd give up one piece and keep two for himself. He rented airplanes to fly him between New York and Chicago, stayed at the Pierre, ate in the best restaurants, wore the finest clothes."

When the feds seized him in 1970 for what they claimed was an excessively larcenous Chicago performance, Raymond was supposed to be held on enormous bail, close to half a million dollars. The authorities there had become somewhat jaded with the act: "They knew he'd been jerking them off," said the FBI agent.

However, Raymond knew how to play Scheherezade. "I can break the Morgan Guaranty Trust case," Raymond told the Chicago authorities. "You cut me loose, I'll set it up through Bayonne Joe [Joe Zicarelli, the New Jersey mob man who appeared to have unlimited access to securities]." It was another spellbinder, too good an opportunity for the FBI to dismiss. Indeed there was nothing to lose. Two agents would accompany Raymond east to make certain that he did not lose his way and be unable to return to Chicago. In addition a number of FBI men from the New York City offices were assigned to the case.

Raymond, befitting his station, ensconced himself at the Plaza in New York. Agents doubtful of Raymond's sincerity became more convinced of his desire to cooperate when the informant arranged a meet at the Oak Room with one of Bayonne Joe's most trusted assistants, a dandified little man with a hawkish face. While Raymond and Bayonne Joe's emissary chatted over their drinks, a number of FBI agents attempted to impersonate other customers in the Oak Room.

Suddenly, Raymond and his guest paid their check and

left for another watering hole, Trader Vic's. "When you're on a surveillance like this," said an FBI agent who worked this case, "you have to move when the subject moves. You can't take a chance on losing him and that means running out of the place without paying the check. We took off after them and left behind us a bad scene with the waiters calling the cops because we seemed to have stiffed them. At least we got away without being arrested. Later, things were squared with the bar; but I know of times where the agents lost their guy because the waiters grabbed the agents when they tried to chase out of a place."

Raymond and his companion reached an agreement for a transaction to be culminated at a restaurant in New Jersey. Raymond's part was that of middleman. The actual buyer was none other than Tony Rose of the FBI, who had posed so successfully as the purchaser with Samuel Schwartz.

Because the restaurant lay in a jurisdiction beyond that of New York City, the local FBI office in the area had to be notified. In turn, the local police chief was told about the caper to prevent any accidental interruption of the scenario. The restaurant that night was a honeycomb of FBI agents and other lawmen waiting for Raymond and Bayonne Joe's rep. There were more feds on hand than customers. However, the distinction quickly became muted. "We were all on the arm," said an agent who participated. "Raymond and his guy were supposed to be there around eight o'clock at night. But they didn't show until a couple of hours later. Our guys had been putting drinks away all the time. They were getting pretty loud, staggering a little.

"Finally, Raymond showed up with his rooster friend and Tony Rose. They sat at the bar bullshitting over a few drinks while our people continued to get loaded. One of the local cops assigned to the place through the police chief sat at the bar drinking gallons of Fresca, which in itself ought to have wised up Bayonne Joe's fellow. But worse, there's suddenly a page for this character; a waiter walks around asking for 'Sgt. Walker, call for Sgt. Walker.' And at one end of the bar, two agents have become so stoned that they've forgotten where they are. They get in a loud conversation about transfers to the Kansas City office and to the office in St. Louis. Still, Bayonne Joe's man does not panic.

"However, one of the agents from Chicago, Bob White-house, was not accustomed to this kind of work. He had been awake for nearly twenty-four hours while this thing was being set up and with all that booze in him he was stoned. Whitehouse stumbled up to the bar where these three guys are and said, 'Hey, when's this whole thing coming down?'

"Bayonne Joe's guy instantly caught on to the situation. He turned to Tony Rose. 'What are you, a cop?' To Raymond he snarled, 'You trying to set me up?'

"Raymond and Rose hustled the rooster off to the men's room to try to cool things," explained the agent. "Myself, I tried to block the path to the men's room after they go inside so that nobody will interrupt them while Raymond and Rose try to pacify the rooster. But Whitehouse now felt an urgent call to nature. He shoved past me into the men's room just as Tony Rose tried to cover for Mike Raymond by throwing a tantrum at Bayonne Joe's boy. 'Who you callin' a cop,' Rose said and he tossed a punch at the rooster. He missed but in the struggle they bumped into Whitehouse who's fumbling with his zipper at the urinal. Whitehouse staggered and wet the front of his pants. Whitehouse reeled out of the men's room with his trouser front soaked, plastered to his leg. 'I don't go for this hard sell bullshit,' he said. 'I'm taking myself off the case,' which is not FBI talk. Agents neither assign themselves to nor relieve themselves from cases.

"That broke the whole thing down. Everybody scattered. At the office it was known as the 'Whitehouse ploy'—if you're burned as an agent by a suspect, you hide your identity by pissing in your pants, like no FBI agent would be expected to. Personally, I don't think Mike Raymond had any hook into the Morgan Guaranty Trust robbery. He is just a guy who likes to talk big, drop names."

On the other hand, it's entirely possible that Bayonne Joe could have been part of the chain for the Morgan Guaranty Trust loot. But the opportunity through Raymond disappeared. That did not discourage Raymond from continuing in his career. He was one of the more voluble witnesses to appear before the Senate Subcommittee, spewing names and incidents, some of whose principals hotly denied their involvement or the facts as recalled by Raymond. In 1974, an enormous fraud involving computerized checks and the City of Los Angeles surfaced. Close to $1,000,000 in checks were cashed before the authorities arrested a pair of well-known swindlers. A few weeks after the story broke it was revealed that the government investigation had been aided by one Michael Raymond who had officially received $43,000 for his services as an informer.

During the first year after the Morgan Guaranty crime, other good Samaritans on the order of Mike Raymond came forward. A Boston attorney who had been a go-between for return of stolen securities was contacted by a New York lawyer named Donald Armstrong. The New Yorker said a caller to his office offered to return T bill number 101719A plus an additional $3.7 million more if an adequate "finder's fee" would recompense him for his troubles.

Armstrong was advised to take up the matter with Henry Rohlf. The Morgan Guaranty Trust vice president pointed out that in this particular instance the piece in question had passed its maturity date. At best, Morgan might go for three points. However, in any event, the bank would not simply participate in a buyback. An arrest had to be part of the deal. "Otherwise, it's the same as blackmail," growled Rohlf. Armstrong explained that he did not know the caller; in fact he himself had never spoken to the individual but the message had been taken by Mrs. Armstrong. Rohlf never heard further from Armstrong, whose name cropped up in the Senate Subcommittee hearings. Mike Raymond, for the moment using the pseudonym of George White, said of Armstrong, "He represents many mob people and other criminals, and through his practice has excellent contacts for the direct supply of stolen securities."

Lawyers whose clients include people in possession of ill-gotten paper operate in a fuzzy area. As officers of the court they are obliged not to further any criminal acts. Yet, they have a responsibility to a client and his confidences are privileged. Hank Rohlf received a number of calls from attorneys, inquiring what kind of arrangement could be made if T bills could be recovered. Rohlf stuck to his policy; reward plus arrest. For those who contacted Rohlf, the attorney-client relationship apparently outweighed any considerations of responsibility to the courts. Not a single one of these inquiries resulted in a subsequent call by the intermediary to the FBI, as Rohlf would suggest. Nor did any of these lawyers ever deliver, even without exposing their clients, a piece that they had learned was available.

Then there were the other volunteers, a man in a Tennessee prison who wrote that if he could be freed he would unravel the entire web behind the Morgan Guaranty Trust operation. And a San Diego prison inmate insisted he knew someone in Las Vegas who could break down the whole business. FBI agents interviewed the jailhouse sleuths and concluded that at most they knew some street gossip and at worst only sought to shorten their time.

Agents quietly questioned some Philadelphians about a

trio from Montreal that proposed a land development project at Montego Bay, Jamaica. One of the Canadians had been in touch with a New Jersey resident with impeccable credentials as a provocateur of securities frauds. However, Treasury bills, so far as the FBI could learn, never were proposed as a way to finance the Montego Bay resort.

While the Treasury bills from the theft continued to pop up around the world and the searchers hit one dry hole after another while digging for the culprits, investigators in New York plodded through the "raw data." It was amassed from interviews with employees, employees' gossip, records obtained from public institutions such as New York City police files, and from private sources such as bank statements. "We did a name check through criminal identification," said Joe Leahy. "Typed up 1,100 requests ourselves."

To the searchers, any kind of social aberration might be a clue to the identity of the person. The agents discovered Morgan Guaranty employed a closet swinger; Mr. Milquetoast by day amid the paper warrens of Wall Street became, unknown to his wife, a mod dresser who joyfully prowled the singles bars at night. But aside from this schizoid pattern there was no evidence to connect him with the crime. There were several Morgan workers who had used marijuana. But the leads petered out; no drug involvement of any substance could be discovered.

Police records of Morgan personnel ran from drunk driving to a long-ago homicide. "We looked for people who played the horses, guys who fooled around with women," said Leahy. "You would be surprised what people will tell you about their fellow employees once you start to bullshit with them."

Two individuals interested the investigators more than the others. One man, Alfred Belli, had been employed in the custody department but some months after the crime he quit Morgan Guaranty Trust. Belli established his own retail business, a store selling audio equipment. The detectives were interested in how Belli put together enough capital to strike out on his own; sudden affluence in the wake of a robbery is a klaxon horn for FBI agents. Belli had been raised in one of the neighborhoods associated with organized crime breeding grounds and he admitted to a nodding acquaintanceship with some people pinpointed as part of the underworld cabal.

Feebees burrowed into Belli's background but he continued to come up clean. He had an adequate explanation of the source of his modest capital. He exhibited no irregularities when he sat for the lie detector examination, one of the six hundred polygraphs administered to Morgan employees.

Jerry Lascala, like Belli, also had been brought up in the same grungy section of Manhattan that was a kind of home hive for the worker bees of organized crime. After Lascala went to work for Morgan Guaranty he prospered in the custody section of the bank, and even more so than Belli, he was highly regarded by a number of Morgan executives and by some of the customers as well.

Those references meant less to the FBI than some information that Lascala was known to place an occasional bet with a bookmaker. They secured records of all of his bank deposits and any that might have been made by his wife. Department stores in the area furnished the agents with copies of the Lascala accounts.

Agents began to question Lascala about his travels during a time period wrapped around the heist. The interview uncovered some discrepancies in Lascala's account of his time and the people he saw. The federal hounds sniffed the traces, the pack pursued with full fury. Businesses yielded to the agents statements that detailed any purchases and payments by the Lascala family. Every number

on the telephone company's list of toll calls from the Lascala house was checked out.

In every large office, the Bureau has an agent whose
chief assignment is to persuade businesses to open up
their records on suspects to the FBI. In the event that a
case will depend upon such information, the Bureau later
obtains a legal subpoena for information that it has already
seen. The interest shown in Lascala by the Bureau was
sufficient for Morgan to furlough him indefinitely in March
of 1971.

Lascala sat around his home brooding about his status as
a prime suspect. When Al Belli happened by (they were
long-time friends) and saw a disconsolate Lascala moping
on his front porch, he stopped to chat. Having already quit
the bank, Belli was unaware of Lascala's disgrace. He was
astonished to find his former co-worker a suspect after he
himself had been cleared. Lascala told Belli that the
agents kept asking him about certain people. The names,
said Lascala, were a mystery to him. The Feebees
badgered, then cajoled: Hadn't Lascala met with D and F,
organized crime hands? The investigators refused to believe Lascala when he claimed that he did not know the
pair nor had he ever held any conversations with anyone
by that name. Belli sympathized with Lascala and said,
"Hell, I know F. It's me they should suspect."

As soon as Belli drove off, Lascala bounded into the
house and telephoned Agent George Binney to report his
conversation with Belli. Binney politely listened, but the
Bureau had already gone through Belli's history and activities and given him a pass.

The FBI continued to ask if Lascala knew a particular
cocktail lounge in the Bay Ridge section of Brooklyn, and
when he answered that he knew nothing of the place the
agents gave him a sorrowful, we know better buddy, ex-
pression. Other Morgan employees were cozened into

confidences about Lascala. Did he have a girl friend, somebody at the office, maybe he slipped out with her for a drink after work? Agents obtained receipts for gasoline bought by Lascala with a credit card; they hoped to find purchases in the targeted area in Brooklyn. But they were disappointed to discover that all of Lascala's gas on credit came from his neighborhood service stations. Any Bay Ridge purchases must have been for cash.

His wife, Ann Lascala, lost her patience with the ever-polite agents who questioned her. She visited the offices of Morgan Guaranty to protest the inquisition visited upon her husband. The nominally placid Lascala, after his suspension from Morgan Guaranty stretched into six weeks, raged at agent Binney, "What are you doing about this! When can I go back to work! I put too many years into this job to see it go down the drain." Binney was an agent who had lost his composure only on one occasion. When chasing a felon at an airport, the blast from a jet aircraft engine had whisked his toupé off. Now, Binney counseled Lascala to have patience. If he were innocent he had nothing to fear; if guilty, however, he would be found out and the punishment would be all the more severe for his failure to cooperate. The FBI wanted very much to pile up points with Morgan Guaranty through identification of The Person. Even more so, the Bureau panted with the desire to establish the route of the paper from The Person to its various destinations around the world. It was back to the polygraph machine for Jerry Lascala. For the investigators it was a dyspeptic diet of frustration.

XIV
The Chase Manhattan Banker Caper

On March 2, 1971, at the federal courthouse in Manhattan's Foley Square began a trial that epitomized a number of facets in the Morgan Guaranty Trust Company robbery. The proceedings illuminated not only the difficulties in efforts to unravel who did what and how, but not so incidentally showed the way the judicial system works, or slips a cog according to one's ideas on justice.

Facing a jury of their peers were Estyne and Joel West, man and wife for about three years. She was five-foot-seven, had hazel eyes, black hair, and was born in Chicago in 1933. Her maiden name was Iris Fishberg but she also went by the name of Estyne Bernsardt and Estyne Del Rio. Her husband, a New Yorker named Joel Wisotsky at birth, was nine years younger, five-foot-seven and 140 pounds. Even before marriage they had created a business office for an import-export enterprise known as Jo Del Consolidated. Their chief accusers were two men, Grant Scruggs and Henry Schumer, who alleged that the Wests tried to use them to negotiate bills that belonged to the Morgan Guaranty loot.

For the government, Patrick Burke of the Eastern District Joint Strike Force opened the trial. "Basically, the government charges that these two defendants [the Wests] conspired to, and actually did, transfer almost $1,000,000 worth of stolen U.S. Treasury bills, in fact, $900,000 worth of stolen U.S. Treasury bills.

"Now one doesn't pass a stolen Treasury bill in the same manner that one would pass a stolen radio, let's say. You just don't walk up to someone on the street and say, 'I've got a radio,' and try to sell it at a discount."

Burke than narrated his version of how the defendants came to be accused. He told the court about Stayne Medical Company, a British-owned manufacturer of medical supplies with a plant in New Jersey. Self-employed Grant Scruggs, described as a "management consultant" and at other times as an "import-export broker," according to Pat Burke, had been contacted by Stayne Medical which wished to sell three million glass syringes. Grant Scruggs advertised these items in foreign newspapers—the *Dawn Press* in Karachi, Pakistan, was one—and he also offered them in Colombia. Burke explained that Scruggs formed an alliance with the Wests who boasted of extensive contacts in Ghana, which was in the market for glass syringes. The Wests, said the prosecutor, handed to Scruggs a $500,000 Treasury bill and three $100,000 ones for payment. An officer of the Chase Manhattan Bank discovered that the T bills were among those reported stolen by the Morgan Guaranty Trust Company and Scruggs was arrested on January 28, 1970.

Burke then recounted a second incident in which the Wests were said to have tried to pass another stolen bill. In this case the recipient was Henry Schumer, a broker for an over-the-counter securities firm. Schumer also discovered that the T bill he obtained from the Wests was one of the missing pieces from Morgan Guaranty. Joel West was then arrested on March 17, 1970, his wife nearly a month later.

In his initial remarks, defense counsel for Joel West, attorney Joseph Rao, foretold how the war for the hearts and minds of the jury would be waged. "Now Mr. Scruggs is going to testify for the prosecution and a man by the name of Mr. Schumer is going to testify for the prosecution. You cannot fault the prosecution, you cannot fault the FBI. They must present a case that is given them and it has been given to them by Scruggs and by Schumer [Rao had dropped the honorifics] and based on their testimony you are expected to determine whether or not Mr. West and Mrs. West are innocent.

"We will show during the course of this trial the type of men who will be making the accusation." Concluded Rao, "You can believe these witnesses or whether or not these witnesses had reason to lie, had motive to lie, had lied before, are lying now and are nothing but inveterate liars. But they are shrewd and they are clever."

Salvatore Nigrone represented Mrs. West. "We will endeavor to prove the shoddy character of the major government witnesses. The news media recently have indicated to all of us that some questionable witnesses are presented by the government in major cases." It was a variation of the credibility attack; in effect, Would you buy a used car from your present government?

The jury was spared an involved presentation on how the Treasury bills came to be missing from the Morgan Guaranty Trust when the defense agreed to the stipulation that there had indeed been a theft of $13,198,000 from the bank. (The apparent $4,000 differential between this sum and the $13,194,000 was caused by the discovery that about three months before the Mets won the World Series, four $1,000 notes had been taken. Possibly that robbery was a damp run for the big score in October.) The defense also accepted the crime was a federal offense and therefore the U.S. District Court had jurisdiction.

Grant Scruggs, a Nebraska native who once reached the U.S. Olympics trials for sprints, went on the witness stand. Through a mutual friend, testified Scruggs, he had been introduced to the Wests, who lived in a spacious apartment in a building on the corner of Fifth Avenue and Sixty-third Street, definitely in the highest rent district of New York City. Grant Scruggs observed on his visits six color telephones around the large room set aside as an office. There was also an international telex machine, copying devices, a small laboratory adjacent, opulent furnishings, and a painting by Xavier Cugat on the wall. Scruggs, who had imported some prefabricated homes to the United States and other countries, told the court he had hopes of supplying this type of housing to Ghana. "Mr. West informed both Mr. Starr [the friend] and myself while we were in the apartment that he had the ability to deliver housing contracts to people who would supply prefabricated buildings for the country of Ghana."

The project seemed to be simply one of a number of propositions that bounced between the Wests and Scruggs. The accused couple tried to interest Scruggs in finding the money to finance a film about Ghana. And then Scruggs, who had been approached by Stayne Medical, broached the possibility of the glass syringes as an item for export to Ghana. In August of 1969 Scruggs said he delivered a sample of the product to the Wests who continually talked of checking things out with "their people." The glass syringes were available at bargain prices, 70 percent below their nominal cost. It was a closeout on the items because the U.S. and other industrialized nations now used only disposable syringes.

The matter seemed to lay dormant until shortly before Christmas of 1969, about two months after the theft of the T bills from Morgan. At that time, said Scruggs, the Wests called him to report their people were in the United States and ready to deal on the glass syringes.

Scruggs now testified that the executives of Stayne while eager to make a sale were concerned that the negotiations be backed by paper. "I was constantly being asked for some indication of good faith from the Ghanians." What Stayne wanted to see was a letter of credit extended to Scruggs or the company he represented, something that showed that there were adequate funds available once a price was agreed upon. The witness said he urged the Wests to obtain from their people something to convince Stayne an actual buyer was at hand.

Grant Scruggs then visited his local banker, James Cooke, who was a second vice president of the Chase Manhattan branch on West Fifty-seventh Street. Scruggs had occasionally gone to the bank for financing and he also knew Cooke slightly as a result of their both being members of the New York Athletic Club. Banker Cooke was treasurer of the NYAC. Scruggs earned his ticket of admission to the rarefied atmosphere of the white-on-white NYAC through membership on its track team.

Cooke advised that he would be willing to issue a letter of credit to Scruggs if a letter of credit from the Ghanians could be proffered to back up the deal. Under the guidance of prosecutor Burke, Scruggs reiterated that he prodded the Wests for either a cash advance from "their people" or a financial instrument acceptable to the bank. Stayne also constantly pushed for something "tangible as an indication of good faith." While the Wests promised an official order for syringes, they failed to deliver one or any material sign of genuine interest by the Ghanians.

With the Ghanians allegedly in New York City, the

Wests urged Scruggs not to take a Christmas vacation with his family to South Dakota. Obligingly, his wife and children flew off without him. Scruggs then related to the court the details of an agreement he made with the Wests in the glass syringe deal. The partners would split evenly the difference between what they paid Stayne for the glass syringes and the price agreed upon by Ghana. At last, Scruggs told the court, the Wests produced for him to show Stayne an order from the firm of Cherub Limited in Ghana for 3,300,000 glass syringes of the sample type.

Toward the end of January, 1970, Scruggs was, he said, told to telephone the New York Hilton and ask for a Mr. Afframs, a Ghanian, who would confirm the order. As a result of this conversation, a car with a Mr. Charlassa, who was supposed to be the representative for Afframs, picked him up the following day. Also in the party was an executive of Stayne Medical, a man named O'Connell. The trio drove out to the New Jersey factory to inspect the glass syringes. There were now only 2.3 million remaining in the inventory. At the factory, the visitors examined and discussed the crating and special packing that the materials required. Out of earshot of Charlassa, Stayne offered to trim its prices for Grant Scruggs. The alleged buyers drove back to New York City.

On January 26, 1970, Scruggs said he met Charlassa at the Hilton. (An FBI investigation, however, found no one registered under this name at the hotel during the period in question. However, Afframs was a real person living in Ghana. There is no sign that the investigators tried to learn from Afframs whether he knew any of the individuals involved and what he might know of the alleged syringe deal.)

The exporter told the court that the available glass syringes now totaled 1.8 million. That evening, said Grant Scruggs, he talked again with Joel West and requested a letter of credit because the executives at Stayne had become weary of talk without any tangible sign of financial interest. The cost of the 1,800,000 syringes to Scruggs and West amounted to only $200,000 The order from Cherub, the Ghana company, figured at $889,000 or a $689,000 profit (less the shipping expenses) to be split by the two Americans. (It was an exorbitant profit, but Stayne wanted to wipe out its inventory.) West, said Scruggs, assured him that the letter of credit would be available on the following day.

Instead, maintained Scruggs, "I received four Treasury notes, one for $500,000 and three for $100,000. He [West] said these were better than a letter of credit, they were comparable to cash. He said to take them into the bank and that I could use these bills to set up a letter of credit." To Scruggs, the T bills looked like "large dollars."

According to the witness, he received the T bills around five in the afternoon, too late to go to his bank. Instead he went to the New York Athletic Club, searching for his acquaintance James Cooke from Chase Manhattan. "He [Cooke] was involved in a formal dinner," remembered Scruggs; but Cooke agreed to confer on the following day. "In the morning, I took the Treasury bills in to the Chase Manhattan Bank and asked Mr. Cooke if it would be possible to set up a letter of credit or some form of payment so that I could now purchase the syringes from Stayne Medical, who had only given us until I think it was 12 noon that day to purchase the syringes.

"Mr. Cooke called down to his central office and it was learned that the bills were stolen and at that point he called the FBI." FBI agents Andy Watson and Homer Hoffman, Jr., took Scruggs into custody. Later in his testimony, Scruggs changed the sequence of events to say that he left the bank for a short time after delivering the T bills in order to have photocopies made of the order from Cherub and his letter to Stayne.

Joseph Rao, the attorney for the defense, now cross-examined Scruggs. "Do you recall that you were questioned by the FBI on the twenty-eighth of January, 1970? . . . Did you tell the FBI that on a recent trip to Europe and on a stopover in London you met two Ghanians named Mr. Bonsu and Mr. Kofon who were associated with Macab International Limited of Accra, Ghana?"

After Scruggs answered yes, Rao developed that when interrogated by the FBI, Scruggs had told the agents that the order for the glass syringes had come from these two Ghanians. In addition, the FBI interview (to which defense counsel had access in the normal course of preparing its case) revealed that Scruggs had never spoken about anyone named Afframs. The FBI notes also contradicted Scruggs in court. Previously he said that Charlassa telephoned his office from the Hilton, rather than that the American contacted the representative from Ghana on his own initiative. Most important for Rao's client, the counselor demonstrated that Scruggs never mentioned the name of Joel West to the FBI during these first sessions of questioning.

Rao also discovered discrepancies in the testimony given by Scruggs to the grand jury and to the court. To the former he reported that he never actually saw James Cooke at the NYAC because the banker was already at dinner. On this point, when the FBI notes of the interview were read by Rao, Scruggs insisted that the FBI memorandums were inaccurate.

The defense asked what Scruggs knew about the import licenses required for Ghana. Did Scruggs, the import-export specialist, not realize that Ghana levied heavy tariffs on medical imports? Scruggs stubbornly rebutted that he believed West with his connections in Ghana could take care of any such problems.

In a standard courtroom tactic, Rao fired a series of incriminating questions at the witness. "Did you know Mr. Schumer?" No! "Did you hire Mr. Charlassa to go to Stayne Medical in New York and represent himself as a buyer for Ghana?" No. "Would you accuse Mr. West of giving you $800,000 worth of T bills if in fact he had not?"

"No, sir."

"Would you accuse Mr. West of committing a criminal act if in fact he was innocent?"

"I can't accuse anybody of anything."

"Would you, sir, accuse Mr. West—not anybody—Mr. West, of committing a criminal act if in fact he was innocent?"

"No, sir, I would not."

"Mr. Scruggs, did you not accuse Charlassa [to the FBI] of giving you these $800,000 worth of T bills when in fact he did not?"

"Yes, sir."

"And did you not accuse Mr. Charlassa of committing a criminal act when in fact he was innocent?"

"No, sir."

"Did you accuse him of giving you $800,000 worth of Treasury bills, sir?"

"No, sir. I stated that he had given them to me."

"You stated he did, did you not?"

"There is a difference between stated and an accusation." Pat Burke rose to defend his witness who had been reduced to semantic explanations of his dissimilar accounts to the initial FBI interrogators and his words in the court. Burke advised the judge that Scruggs's earliest version failed to mention the Wests because he was afraid of them and thought they had underworld connections. Rao objected strongly to using the "underworld nonsense" and insisted that Scruggs fingered the Wests because "he was bailing himself out."

Burke on redirect examination got Scruggs to say, "I think the only way to describe [my state of mind with the FBI] is just about total numbness of the events at that time. I was afraid to implicate the real . . . I realized who were the real people behind this whole thing."

After Scruggs, members of the supporting cast appeared on the witness stand. John Willey, president of Stayne, recapitulated his conversations with Scruggs. None of his testimony incriminated the accused couple. Rao asked few questions. "And you say that he [Scruggs] introduced you to a man whose name was Mr. Charles?"

"I have his card somewhere. But don't hold me to that name. I think his last name was Charles, as I recall, because I remember Ezzard Charles the fighter, and he looked like him."

James Cooke, beefy, mustachioed, with the pomposity befitting a Chase Manhattan second vice president ("a walking caricature of a banker," says Pat Burke), took the witness stand. Cooke supported Scruggs's story to some extent. He told the court that he did meet with Scruggs in the lobby of the New York Athletic Club on the night in question. Cooke described the process by which it was learned that the $800,000 in T bills were stolen. Unable to authenticate the certificates at his own branch office, Cooke reported, "We tried to get somebody downtown at Chase to check the numbers, and eventually I checked with the Federal Reserve Bank and we found that the numbers agreed with some stolen bonds." Obviously, the banking community occupied itself with other matters than keeping track of ill-gotten securities.

With Cooke on the stand, Burke prepared the way for the introduction of his second principal witness against the Wests. He drew from the Chase Manhattan's second vice president that he had known Henry Schumer for twenty-five years, and then he asked the banker to describe events that began a few weeks after Grant Scruggs presented his T bills. On February 19, Cooke reported that Henry Schumer approached him. "He said he had been talking to a gentleman that was going to offer him one $1,000,000 and two $100,000 Treasury certificates and I suggested if possible to get the numbers and we would check them." The proposition was to borrow money against these securities. Roughly one month later, said the banker, Schumer returned to Cooke's office and handed over a $100,000 Treasury bill.

"Well, I called down to the Federal Reserve and spoke to a Mr. Debs. We gave him the number and he said, 'Well, it is only one number out of the way.' And he mentioned the number and it looked like the fifth number should have been a zero. It is now a nine. It has been changed to a nine." A zero would give the T bill the same number as was on one of the purloined items.

Joseph Rao cross-examined Cooke about the laws of probability and coincidence. Cooke admitted that within New York City there must be at least a thousand banks and yet it happened that within a few short weeks Cooke was approached twice. "It is coincidental, is it not Mr. Cooke, that two separate individuals with stolen securities have the same bank vice president in Manhattan?" Cooke also admitted that before he received the bill from Henry Schumer he had given him a list of numbers for stolen Treasury bills. Rao was trying to get the jury to infer that knowing which numbers were recorded as stolen, Schumer could have been the one to make a nine out of a zero.

Several FBI agents testified after Cooke stepped down. Joel West had been arrested March 17 by Special Agent Andy Watson and another FBI man in the offices of Schumer. Although Estyne West was present then, no warrant for her was issued until two days later. She disappeared for a few weeks before voluntarily surrendering, accompanied by counsel, at the offices of a U.S. Commissioner.

The court listened to a brief argument over why Estyne West, now a defendant, had not been seized with her husband. The government witnesses contended that Schumer actually received the T bill from Joel West, but it was learned later she had participated in the negotiations that preceded the scene at James Cooke's branch of the Chase Manhattan.

FBI Agent Robert J. Hazen was summoned to the witness chair for his bureaucratese testimony. "Included amongst my official duties were the examination of fragmentary latent prints which may be either present or possibly developed on objects which are associated with various types of crime. I also make comparison of inked prints and latent prints and as a member of the FBI Disaster Squad on occasion I will examine the hands of unknown deceased individuals in an attempt to establish their identity."

Special Agent Hazen then said he matched a print from the hand of Joel West with a latent print on Treasury bill 1017848A. For the benefit of any doubters he described the characteristics where ridges on West's fingers join, where ridges end, the relations to other ridges, all of which added up to the singular configuration belonging to Joel West. On 1017936A and 1017759A, $100,000 notes, and 104540A, a $500,000 note, Hazen detected the mark of Estyne West.

Henry Schumer, who had at one time run Schumer Theatrical Trucking which transported scenery for almost all of the New York City theatrical productions, began his testimony by telling the court that a friend in the trucking business had suggested he might, in his new capacity as a stockbroker, find some profitable undertaking in concert with the Wests. They were strangers to Schumer but their secretary telephoned Schumer to arrange a meeting. After several false starts the Wests invited Henry Schumer to their Fifth Avenue and Sixty-third Street apartment on February 20, 1970. Over cocktails they exchanged inconsequential chatter over their experiences abroad. The ritual of pre-business sparring over, said Schumer, they got down to the proposition. Joel West wished to negotiate an immediate loan of $1,000,000 and if Schumer would serve as the broker between the financial institution and West, his commission would be $200,000. The collateral for the loan would be more than $1,000,000 in Treasury bills.

"He told me the source of the T bills came from a chemical company in Lucerne, Switzerland, and that they were given to him for a mercury patent that he had for extruding mercury from ore, which was the greatest invention ever created.

"The purpose of the loan was to buy uncut diamonds. He was expecting an immediate shipment and needed the cash immediately. We first discussed that due to certain transactions that he had in Switzerland, he wasn't allowed to show the money here because he couldn't declare it. The entire transaction had to be done very quietly and his name couldn't be mentioned in it. These were the reasons that he couldn't cash in the bills.

"Why don't you take them in, any bank would allow 90 percent of a loan and you would not have to give a $200,000 commission?" Schumer told the court he advised West.

"What was his answer?"

"That he couldn't do it on account of tax purposes. Number two, that he was associated with Switzerland, and number three that he was associated with Ghana and Israel and all that money could not be shown."

Schumer claimed that he questioned West about the collateral. "I asked were the Treasury bills legitimate ones?
Were they in any way connected with the Mafia or any
mobs, or were they stolen? I said if they were, don't even
discuss it any further with me because I am not interested
in it."

Supposedly West swore that the Treasury bills were absolutely authentic and untouched by any taint of illegality.
In fact, he said, testified Schumer, that they actually came
from Dow Chemical Company's Swiss offices in payment
for the discovery of the mercury ore process.

Shortly thereafter, Henry Schumer paid a call on his
banker, James Cooke at the Fifty-seventh Street branch of
the Chase Manhattan Bank. "I mentioned Ghana to him
and he started to laugh. He said this is the second transaction in which Ghana was mentioned. 'I can't believe this.
There is another depositor, another customer at the bank,
who just had a transaction involving $800,000 in Treasury
bills and also had something to do with Ghana.' " According to the witness, the banker immediately obtained a list
of numbers for stolen Treasury bills and warned, "Hank,
be very, very careful and check it out very carefully."

Schumer met with West again. This session was at the
broker's apartment, which was not far from that of the
Wests. They talked of other business propositions. A
friend of Schumer was anxious to procure a license to sell
business machines in Ghana. West assured his host that
such permission could be easily negotiated. But for the
moment, Schumer said, he was told the Treasury bills
needed to back the loan desired by West had been tied up
in an escrow account at a Fifth Avenue bank.

The interplay between them continued with another
conversation in Schumer's office at First William Company,
99 Park Avenue. On this occasion West brought with him a
brown envelope. Over a lunch of sandwiches, Joel West,

said Schumer, painted a heady picture of big-time financial coups in Ghana, of building warehouses and apart-
ments, of importing various kinds of business machines, of
film properties. He sketched out on a piece of paper a kind
of table of organization for these investments in which
Henry Schumer occupied a high executive position.

"He also was telling me of the urgency to get to Ghana
as fast as possible because there was a change in the government that would be very favorable." For this quick maneuver, West said he needed $50,000 to $60,000 and with
that he opened the envelope and produced a sheaf of stock
certificates one and one-half inches thick." Schumer said
he examined the securities—stock in Westinghouse,
AT&T, and Singer—which represented perhaps three-
quarters of a million in blue chips and they all bore the
street name, Glore, Forgan and Staats. (Stocks that bear
the name of a brokerage firm rather than that of individual
customers are in street names.)

Again it would appear obvious that no intermediary
would be necessary to float a relatively small percentage of
the market value backed by these items. However,
Schumer said that West felt this avenue was closed to him
because these had all belonged to his wife and had been
in the wife's family for a long, long time. (Apparently, like
jewelry and antiques, it's possible to consider stocks as
heirlooms.) He did not want to sell any of it now, particularly because of taxes—a little less sentiment, a bit more
fiscal know-how.

Schumer was a newcomer to the brokerage business and
he advised his customer that there ought not to be any
problem, if the certificates could be properly authenticated. And that would require only a moment to check.
Schumer trotted off to see the president of his firm and
learned that there was no way First William would touch
these pieces. Stocks held in street name ordinarily never

leave the premises of the company in whose name they are held. On the books of Glore, Forgan and Staats there would be, for example, the ten names of customers holding perhaps 1,000 shares a piece of IBM. Rather than retain possession of individual pieces for these shareholders, for whom it acted as the guardian of the assets, Glore, Forgan and Staats held 10,000 shares in its street name. It was a technique that simplified the paper chase and the storage space for Wall Street firms. But it is uncommon for private individuals to be lawfully in possession of certificates listed in street names and then only if a proper endorsement has been recorded on the backs of the certificates. The advice given to Schumer to pass along to his client was that in order to negotiate the securities they would have to be authenticated and proof of ownership shown.

West responded, "That is no problem. I will be back in half or three-quarters of an hour." But, said Schumer, West never returned to the office that day nor did he call. However, two days later he received a call to meet Joel West at a Chase Manhattan Bank at Forty-fifth and Madison. The word was that the attorney for the Wests had retrieved the $1.2 million in Treasury bills formerly in escrow and Mrs. West would deliver them to Schumer and West at the Chase Manhattan offices. The two men waited for forty-five minutes but Mrs. West failed to arrive. Her husband visited his vault in the bank's basement. He flashed a Treasury bill, claimed Schumer. After an hour passed a breathless Estyne West rushed into the bank to announce excitedly that the attorney had been in a car accident and unfortunately the Treasury bills had been forced to accompany him to the hospital.

Schumer, somewhat miffed by the constant delays, departed while husband and wife argued over the latest misadventure.

Some four days later, Schumer reported that he received a telephone call from Mrs. West in which she announced that her husband now had possession of the $100,000 Treasury bill on which he proposed to float a loan. He expected to go to Ghana immediately after receipt of the money. Schumer's commission was to be the difference between the loan (in the neighborhood of $50,000 to $60,000) and the actual value of the Treasury bill, which would probably be in the mid-$90,000 range. At 8:30 one evening a few days later, the doorbell of the Schumer apartment rang and Henry Schumer clad in his pajamas and robe found the Wests on his doorstep, accompanied by their small poodle. The visitors had combined the need for an evening constitutional for the poodle with the task of handing over the Treasury bill. Schumer accepted the certificate in the foyer of his apartment. Since his wife was not feeling well, he did not invite the Wests into the apartment. But the poodle slipped into the living room where Schumer's wife and child admired it for a moment.

On the following day, Schumer met with James Cooke at the Chase Manhattan Bank where the two men studied the Treasury bill and, as Cooke had previously testified, both discerned alterations in the serial number. FBI Special Agent Andy Watson answered a call to the Agency. After consultation with Watson it was agreed that Schumer should telephone West to meet him at his First William Company offices, ostensibly to receive the proceeds of the loan. When West arrived, with his wife, the husband was placed under arrest.

That completed Schumer's direct examination by Pat Burke, and Joseph Rao began his cross-examination. He led Schumer through his downward spiraling business career, from theatrical trucking magnate to stockbroker to the current job of sales manager for the truck leasing division of a Florida company. Rao asked if it were customary for

Schumer to discuss $1,200,000 deals on the telephone, and then openly tried to demolish the credibility of Schumer. Why hadn't the broker said "no deal" when it became obvious that West was trying to avoid income tax?

"I fail to see how I'd become part of the conspiracy [to avoid income tax]," replied the witness.

"You were a financial consultant. Do you think this is very ethical?"

U.S. Attorney Burke objected and Judge Edward Weinfeld sustained. The judge added, "As a matter of fact, tax avoidance is not a crime. It is tax evasion, willful tax evasion, that is a crime," Judge Weinfeld reminded the jury.

Rao pecked away at Schumer's willingness to be a party to strange financial deals. The witness admitted that he thought the story about the uncut diamonds was "farfetched" but "one out of a million might be true."

"As a matter of fact you didn't believe him . . . you thought that it was incredible?" In traditional adversarial cross-examination style, Rao couched what were supposed to be questions in accusatory assertions.

"Yes."

"You thought that it was a phony deal?"

"Yes."

"And yet you kept dealing with a man who had related a story to you that you considered was incredible, phony, farfetched, you didn't believe him and you kept dealing with this man?"

"Yes, sir. Why don't you ask me why?" Rao immediately objected to the witness's try to guide his inquisition and Judge Weinfeld supported him.

Rao drew Schumer back to the scene at the First William Company when Joel West supposedly handed him the sheaf of stock certificates in the name of Glore, Forgan and Staats. How was it that Schumer the broker was so unknowing about the negotiability of the items?

"I wasn't completely aware of exactly what a certificate is, in order to be completely authenticated and passable by various brokerage houses. This we leave to the cage." (Schumer had actually only been in the business for a few months.)

"So you realized after the conference with the president of the company," said Rao, "that since these stocks were in street name, the only way they could be released from a brokerage house would be if there were proper stock authentication, to wit, the name of the transfer agent and proof of ownership?"

"No, there are occasions where they are sometimes released in street name." (But not without endorsement.)

"Was it obvious to you that these stocks were stolen?"

"No, sir."

"Is it your testimony that it was obvious to you that the stocks were not stolen?"

"Yes."

Rao then read from the minutes of Schumer's testimony to the grand jury. "I took the stock into the president of the company, Jack Portnoy, and we looked at it. And all the stocks were in what we call street name, in the name of a brokerage house, Glore, Forgan and Staats and if you know anything about stocks, on the back of the stock anytime that a stock is released in street name it must have authentication, the transfer agent and usually proof of ownership. These stocks were either stolen or there is no other way of getting it into the hands of an individual unless they are taken out of an office.

"So I showed it to the president of the company and he said he didn't like the looks of it. He said, 'Tell him to get them authenticated and proof of ownership and we might be able to do something.'"

Rao concluded the reading and commented, "So it was obvious that these stocks were stolen? Wasn't it?"

The court record indicates that Schumer failed to answer. Rao pressed him again, "Wasn't it?"

Schumer doggedly answered, "Not really."

Rao developed that the simplest way to have determined the legitimacy of ownership would have been by a telephone call from Schumer to Glore, Forgan and Staats. The witness admitted, "That was the stupidest thing I ever did, not making that telephone call."

Rao elicited another tidbit of information. Schumer admitted he had not given the Wests a receipt for the $100,000 T bill, which, considering the easy negotiability of such a certificate smacks of sloppy procedures. The defense lawyer drew the information that Schumer had previously been employed by another brokerage firm and there had been some thefts from that organization. But there was no connection of Schumer to the thefts. He flat-out asked if Schumer had in fact drawn the Glore, Forgan and Staats stock out of his own desk, drawn to show to Joel West. The witness denied the accusation.

Schumer was finished, and Burke brought forward William Yates, director of the patent department for Dow Chemical, as the next prosecution witness. He reported that Dow was not in the mercury extraction business and the company had no record of any payments to either a Joel West or a Joel Wisotsky. Next, a bank employee testified on the safe deposit boxes held by the Wests under the names of Iris Fishberg and Morris Fishberg, and then an expert did a short number on the technique for altering the serial numbers on the T bill.

The defense called its only witness, Joel West himself. Rao navigated his client through his autobiography. He had earned a bachelor of science degree from New York University, done a year of graduate study there, studied at Brooklyn College and Bridgewater State College in Massachusetts in pursuit of a master of science degree. He was still in the process of earning a doctorate on a National Science Foundation scholarship and he had never been arrested before his seizure for the conspiracy to trade the Treasury bills.

Asked if he had held any jobs to support himself while in school, the slightly built West apologized, "I was on the swimming team at college and practicing after school and I didn't have much time for employment. They did give me a job in the cafeteria and in the coat room at school, however.

"I also found time after school to instruct the swimming team at the local Y and to coach and instruct the swimming team there during the summer and I was employed as a life guard at the public beach." He performed that chore for five summers.

Asked Rao, "And during that time what did the records of the park department reflect as to how many lives you in fact saved?"

"One hundred and twenty," matter-of-factly answered West, who also informed the court that he held two intercollegiate swimming records, one for 200 meters and another for the individual medley. (National Collegiate Athletic Association record books for the period fail to show these achievements.)

West said that he had taught high school after he graduated from NYU and supplemented his income through his swimming instruction in the after hours. During his time of trial, he was a teacher at Haaren High School in New York City, and under prodding by his counsel he admitted, "I run the science club at school for the kids. This is an extracurricular activity [for no extra pay]." To make income meet expenditures, West explained, "I presently have an application pending with the New York City Taxi Bureau to drive a cab."

Rao inquired about the invention of which he had spoken to Henry Schumer. West described it as "a process for refining mercury. . . . The process which is used now for refining mercury is what is known as a retort method. It amounts to heating the crude mercury ore in large vats, [from] which large amounts escape into the atmosphere and large amounts into the seas." He explained to the court that this was the source of the mercury contamination for tuna and swordfish. On the other hand, the West method involved what he called a closed system, a chemical way that resulted in no runoff. The process, he said, had been jointly developed with a David Roth, who was supposed to be an employee of the "Howard Hughes organization" and with Dow Chemical as well. Meanwhile, West said he was at work on other inventions including one "I call a terrigation process." Burke objected to the question's relevance and no one in the court, including Joseph Rao, asked what the purpose of "terrigation" was.

The defendant, with the guidance of his lawyer, moved into subjects that had been mentioned earlier in the trial. He and his wife, he said, had visited Ghana for eight weeks beginning in January, 1969. West tried to tell the court of his attempts to export local black opera from Ghana but Burke proffered another objection. Judge Weinfeld agreed. "The charge in this indictment is possession of bonds stolen from a bank that was federally insured and also that the defendants knew the bonds were stolen when they had possession of them."

Rao turned his client's attention to his circumstances at the time of the alleged crime. West told the court that his rent on the Fifth Avenue apartment amounted to $20,000 a year, which would be steep even for a teacher who taught kids how to swim in the afternoon. But it seems that Estyne West whom he married less than three years earlier had created a highly profitable business a few years before, Pedigree Palace, a "dog emporium," the largest in the country, said West, for the grooming of pets. "During that time, during the six months prior to the time that I met her, she had done eighteen TV shows, and had much publicity [in the office of the apartment was a photo of Estyne West with Johnny Carson] in the *Wall Street Journal*." A public company by the name of Meljan Industries, said West, acquired her dog business for $150,000, paying off in stock. An insurance claim had netted $75,000 in cash.

West admitted having discussed business with Grant Scruggs, but contended that his sole interest was in prefabricated housing, for which Ghana had great need. He insisted that Ghanian health authorities sought disposable syringes and were never in the market for the obsolete glass ones. On occasion, said West, Scruggs borrowed the use of the Wests' apartment office to type letters, using the excuse that he was shifting his own quarters at the time and temporarily needed some place to work.

"According to your knowledge," asked Rao, "how much duty must be paid in Ghana on the importation of $899,627 of merchandise?"

"According to the handbook of commerce and industry, what they call in Ghana the Red Book, it is 50 percent duty on pharmaceutical items not under an open license."

West reported that Grant Scruggs actually approached him with another sordid proposition. The management consultant asked if West would "accept Nigerian black market money or money from stolen art to finance the housing project." When West indicated his reluctance toward such an operation, he said Scruggs then showed him $900,000 worth of Treasury bills. "I remember because that is a lot of money." A $500,000 and four $100,000 pieces were what Scruggs supposedly placed on the table.

West explained that his wife happened to enter the room during this conversation. "When my wife saw them, she jumped up and said, 'What, my God, is this?' She touched the notes." West said he also fingered the certificates, which explained the fingerprints described by the FBI agent. As to further involvement with Grant Scruggs and his unusual ways to finance projects, West said, "I had half a heart about the whole thing, I really lost interest."

West now rebutted the testimony of Henry Schumer. Although the latter had denied under oath that he knew Grant Scruggs, West testified that at their very first meeting, Schumer warned him about Scruggs, explaining that he had recently been fired from a job at the Rockefeller Foundation.

The initial proposition, said West, was one created by Schumer. The broker wanted to export typewriters, calculators, adding machines, and similar items to Africa and he sought West's expertise on the area. Schumer supposedly informed West that the operation could be funded through a series of discretionary accounts in Schumer's control. These were customers who gave total custody of their holdings to the broker, who had the power to buy and sell without the need to secure an okay from the individual on each occasion.

Furthermore, said West, on the evening of the poodle walk, it was Schumer who telephoned them and asked the couple to drop by. And it was Schumer who produced the $100,000 Treasury bill which was then fingered by both of the Wests as they examined it. At that time, the Wests agreed to meet at Schumer's office on the following day to conclude a deal that would involve the export of business machines to Africa.

Pat Burke's cross-examination, like that of Joseph Rao, poked into the logic of the witness's story. The U.S. Attorney wanted to know whether it was likely that Henry Schumer would be in pajamas and a robe if he had invited guests to drop by. He thought it strange that Schumer would answer the doorbell with the $100,000 note in hand. West replied that since Schumer had telephoned earlier he must have known who was at the door. Why, asked Burke, did the Wests seek any outside financing for their operations when the gist of West's testimony was that they had almost a quarter of a million in assets? West protested that their capital was tied up largely in stock in Meljan Industries.

Burke shifted to the character of Joel West and the subsequent argument forced the jury to leave the courtroom while the opposing attorneys argued their points before Judge Weinfeld. When Rao asked if West had been arrested prior to this indictment, the witness had answered no. Now Burke wanted to know if West had been arrested subsequent to the indictment. Rao felt that was out of order on the grounds that the defendant should only be questioned on matters up to the time of indictment.

Judge Weinfeld listened briefly to the arguing attorneys and then said, "I think the door has been opened by the question that was put [Have you been arrested before the indictment?]. I think it would clearly go to an issue of credibility. I think it was a deliberate attempt to convey to the jury that this man's life has been blameless as far as the law is concerned."

Rao protested while Burke pointed out that West's high school record, his teaching career, and his deeds as a life guard had all been put before the jury in an attempt to build up credibility for his testimony.

Judge Weinfeld spoke to Rao again, "I mean you were attempting to convey to the jury the fact that the man led a blameless life. I am very much surprised, Mr. Rao, by the manner in which this was handled." The judge reserved his decision on whether Burke could introduce other arrests of West after the indictment. The jury returned. Burke hammered at West's truthfulness. The defendant admitted in court that he had supplied false information on the forms filled out at the Forty-fifth Street branch of the Chase Manhattan Bank, where he had a safe deposit box under the name of Fishberg, and gave a wrong address for himself.

Burke asked West what happened after Schumer showed the couple the $100,000 note and West answered that to his wife he murmured, "Another Scruggs." If, as he had previously testified, West had heard nothing from Scruggs after their last meeting, knew nothing of his arrest, nor knew that the T bills which Scruggs flashed at him had been stolen, why remark "Another Scruggs"?

West rebutted he only meant it was another instance of a promotion backed by Treasury bills and was probably as unsubstantial as Grant Scruggs's.

Judge Weinfeld now sent the jury out of the courtroom again and to the chagrin of Pat Burke announced that he would not permit the prosecutor to introduce witnesses who could show that, subsequent to the indictment, West had been arrested by the New York City Police Department in January of 1971 for grand larceny and forgery in the amount of $59,000 and that one month later the New York cops again had picked him up for possession of stolen stock certificates.

West left the witness stand, and when the jury returned it was addressed by the defense counsel. Salvatore Nigrone, representing Mrs. West, strafed Grant Scruggs, "a man whom the testimony has shown is in debt, a man who is in constant quest of an angle or a deal, a man always looking for a fast buck, and a man who would not have any qualms of conscience in passing a buck." Nigrone cited the various inconsistencies of Scruggs's testimony, particularly his FBI statement which never mentioned either of the Wests. In a penultimate appeal to mercy as well as justice, Nigrone orated, "Whatever the verdict is, you folks

will go home to your family and friends and in time forget
about this trial. But my client will never forget this trial."
And he finished off with a reminder of traditional values in
American jurisprudence: "Better to acquit a hundred
guilty men than it is to convict one innocent man."

Rao was next in summation. He too appealed for delib-
eration that incorporated what are supposedly fundamen-
tal considerations, "presumption of innocence," and "reasonable doubt." Grant Scruggs's character received
another drubbing. Rao's discourse then took a brief surprising turn. "I think one of the finest witnesses I've ever
seen in my life was the FBI agent who testified here and
who told us about the ink impressions [fingerprints]. He
was a fine witness, Mr. Burke, an excellent man. You
should be proud that we have an FBI in this country."
However, Rao did wonder how it was possible that no
fingerprints by Scruggs or Schumer were ever found on
any of the Treasury bills since both testified that they had
handled the bills.

Conceivably, Rao's complimentary remarks about the
Bureau were aimed to counteract any sentiment among the
jury that the FBI's association with the prosecution inevitably connoted the defense's hostility to that organization
so dedicated against crime.

Rao reiterated the unlikely coincidence of two instances
of stolen Treasury bills being presented to the same bank
branch in New York City. He theorized that the scene at
First William Company in which Schumer allegedly conferred with his superiors was simply Schumer's painstak-
ingly constructed alibi for his own larcenous acts. He
dismissed the contradiction of Joel West by the
representative of Dow Chemical, questioning whether the
U.S. officials of the company would be aware of their
Swiss division's actions.

Finally, Rao leaned heavily upon the credibility of his

only witness, who as the lawyer observed was not obliged to testify but took the stand, "out of respect to you, ladies and gentlemen, so you could hear the facts and out of respect for himself and more important he took it out of respect for his wife. He answered for her like a man should, like a man did." It's an interesting argument; any prosecutor who dared to indicate to a jury that a defendant refused to take the witness stand would be faced by a furious defense lawyer objecting to any inference being drawn against an individual exercising his constitutional rights. In many cases, when a judge charges the jury he will specifically admonish the panel not to draw any conclusions because the defendant did not choose to testify. Rao thus made a great virtue out of an act for which there is no converse sin.

In his summation, Burke tried to shore up the credibility of his two major witnesses. He noted that Scruggs had tried to obtain a letter of credit from James Cooke at the Chase Manhattan branch in what would appear to be a genuine business proposition rather than a confidence scheme. Burke questioned whether supposed swindlers—such as the defense made Grant Scruggs and Henry Schumer out to be—would approach their own banker with stolen Treasury bills. He rebutted the Dow Chemical explanation offered by West by reminding the jury that Dow said it was not in the mercury business at all.

Judge Weinfeld in his charge to the jury also concerned himself with credibility, advising Joel West's twelve peers to consider, "demeanor, conduct before you, and whether you are satisfied from his manner that he is telling a truthful story. . . . Did a witness's version appear straightforward and candid or did he try to hide or conceal some of the facts?" Perhaps all prospective jurors might be required to study body language or nonverbal behavior as an aid to determining the veracity of witnesses.

During the trial, the phrase "circumstantial evidence" had been uttered on several occasions. In spite of a number of clichés that label such material as meaningless, it is often quite seriously considered. Judge Weinfeld offered to the jury an example of circumstantial evidence, the case of a windowless courtroom where people arrive with wet raincoats, umbrellas, and "pitter-patter can be heard against the window." (A contradiction in a "windowless courtroom," unless the panes are opaque.) On the basis of this circumstantial evidence, Judge Weinfeld pointed out, it is reasonable to infer that it is raining outside.

Finally, Judge Weinfeld noted that credibility also involves the defendant who testifies in his own behalf. The jury was instructed that a defendant had considerable motive for false testimony but one cannot assume either that the individual lies. Determination again rests chiefly on how the tale is told. And of course, asserted Judge Weinfeld, one was not to infer that because Mrs. West failed to appear as a witness she is guilty.

The jury found Joel and Estyne West not guilty.

In declaring the Wests innocent, the jury chose not to accept the prosecution's web of evidence against them. It believed Joel West rather than Grant Scruggs, Henry Schumer, the FBI, and banker Cooke. And reviewing the trial it's quite apparent that what swung the veniremen and women was the presentation of Joel West—the savior of one hundred and twenty from drowning, a teacher of children, and a softspoken, almost fragile, young man who insisted he was not culpable.

"Nobody got hurt, nobody lost any money," says a former U.S. Attorney acquainted with the case. "The jury saw Joel West, a *nebbish*, on trial and they couldn't see anything to be gained by locking him up."

Pat Burke in retrospect attributes the verdict to some

miscalculations. "I let Rao put all the stuff in about Joel West's character even though I could have stopped it because I believed it opened up the way for me to bring in his subsequent arrests, that he used an alias which he denied he used in court. I think Judge Weinfeld agreed with me, but I think that he figured that the jury would find West guilty anyway and he wanted to avoid any ruling that might lead to a reversal later."

The former Assistant U.S. Attorney admits that he would have preferred a better investigation of the case. The backgrounds of the two chief prosecution witnesses and their accounts were not deeply researched. If Joel West really was involved the agents should have waited until the accused man made some incriminating statements to Henry Schumer at the time they met in Schumer's office subsequent to the broker's presentation of the altered T bill to James Cooke.

The trial left unanswered a $900,000 question: Where did the pieces of Morgan Guaranty loot come from? The recovery of these T bills provided no clues to the route taken, once The Person left the premises of Morgan in October of 1969.

For Joel West, the arrest in connection with this crime was the first in a series of brushes with the law. Only a few days after a jury declared him innocent of wrongdoing with the T bills, Joel West and a companion, Barry Friedman, entered a Chase Manhattan branch office at 726 Madison Avenue in New York. (What would Rao say about this coincidence?) Friedman went to a teller's window and handed her a slip that announced this was a holdup while West lounged unobtrusively nearby. In his pocket was a pistol.

The bank teller managed to trip an alarm. In the ensuing commotion, Friedman was grabbed immediately. West, whose presence had not been announced, probably could have walked out of the bank and escaped unnoticed. Instead he broke into a run. He became the quarry of a chase. Rounding a corner, out of breath, with police sirens in the background, West yanked open the door of a cab where the driver was reading the newspaper. "Let's go," ordered West. The driver, however, continued to study his newspaper until the pursuing cops pulled open the cab door and invited West to emerge.

In addition, West's photograph was shown to witnesses of a bank robbery in Yonkers, New York, that had occurred in December of 1970, and he was identified as a participant in that robbery. West always denied a role in the earlier crime but he pleaded guilty to the second one and served a brief term.

He also subsequently pleaded guilty to charges in early 1971 by the New York City police to possession of stolen stock securities. He received a one-year term. His time was reduced for good behavior. After his release, both he and his wife continued to live in the New York City area.

XV

Last Accounting

Shortly after April 9, 1970, a final accounting of the liability of Morgan Guaranty and its insurers could be toted up. The claims presented for collection at maturity of the notes by "innocent holders in due course" amounted to $723,000 of the $13,194,000 in stolen Treasury bills. The definition of an "innocent holder in due course" was critical in determining who would eventually be stuck for a stolen bill.

In the language of the trade, to qualify as a holder in due course, the transferee must take possession of an instrument that appears to be complete and regular. The stipulation covers improperly drawn papers and counterfeits and it is a responsibility of the holder to make a genuine effort to determine the authenticity of any paper he assumes.

Usually, the holder must take possession before the note becomes overdue or past maturity. The fact that securities are overdue does not automatically deprive a purchaser of a legitimate claim but it can indicate that the items should be scrutinized very carefully as to origins and the title claimed to them by the seller.

The securities must not have been "dishonored," which means that a holder cannot expect to collect on items that have been voided or retired for some reason. The buyer's interest must also be sustained by proof of purchase in good faith and for value. There must have been some quid pro quo to the transaction. Finally, the securities must be bought "without notice of any infirmity in the instrument or defect in the title of the transfer."

"Good faith" and the absence of any "defect in the title of the transfer" were the focal points when Morgan Guaranty contested the claim of innocent holder in due course by several institutions.

For the benefit of Senators and staff on the Permanent Subcommittee on Investigations listening to testimony about fraud and theft in the securities market, then Assistant Attorney General Henry E. Petersen submitted an explanation of the precedents for the terms "good faith" and "innocent holder in due course."

> At common law, the Doctrine of "good faith" was painstakingly developed. Miller v. Race established the free circulation of commercial paper in England in the early 1800's. A series of cases followed, culminating in the celebrated case of Gill v. Cubit, where the Court of King's Bench laid down the rule that reasonable prudence and caution must be exercised by the purchaser and that if circumstances were such as ought to have excited the suspicion of a prudent man and no inquiry were made, then he did not stand in the legal position of a holder in due course. In other words, suspicious circumstances *alone* would let in equities and defenses against such a purchaser. In 1836, England rejected this rule in the case of Goodman v. Harvey, holding that nothing short of actual knowledge of defects or infirmi-

ties would deprive a purchase of the holder in due course status.

In the United States, the several jurisdictions followed a dual line of development. Some followed the former rule of Gill v. Cubit and others followed the rule of Goodman v. Harvey. This dual approach to the problem was finally resolved in 1924 when all the states adopted the Uniform Negotiable Instruments Law (NIL) and this was the law until the adoption of the present Uniform Commercial Code by the states. Under the NIL, to constitute notice of an infirmity, the person to whom the instrument is negotiated "must have actual knowledge of the infirmity or defect or knowledge of such facts that his action in taking the instrument amounts to bad faith."

In the 1952 official draft of the Uniform Commercial Code (UCC), the NIL's "actual knowledge" test of good faith was dropped in favor of a "reasonableness" test of good faith, i.e., "good faith" means "the observance of the reasonable commercial standards of any business in which the holder may be engaged." The Code's comment intimated that a bare showing of "honesty-in-fact" was not enough when a purchaser's actions failed to meet accepted standards.

The banking community strongly objected to this language in the UCC, asserting that it was an attempt to revive the "reasonableness" test of Gill v. Cubit. They felt that such a revival would hamper the free flow of commercial paper and add considerably to their operating costs because of the time and expense necessary in conducting a credit investigation to determine whether or not any infirmities exist in relation to the instrument being negotiated. So much opposition arose that the editorial board of the UCC voted to delete the controversial language.

In place of this unacceptable requirement, the text of the UCC, as Petersen points out, qualifies one as a holder in due course if he assumes a security "in good faith and without notice of adverse claims." Henry Petersen's brief history exposes the basic dilemma of the financial community. The most certain way to limit predators is to demand that every buyer make sure that the seller owns the piece free and clear. However, a regimen that insists upon a thorough investigation of the title of every paper instrument negotiated impedes the flow of paper fodder. And modern finance has an almost insatiable appetite that can be appeased only by enormous turnover.

The problem with the "reasonableness" test is that in practice it is indefinable. How extensive must a title search be to qualify as "reasonable"? Or, more to the point, when would the customer become annoyed by the delays and go elsewhere with his business?

Discarding "reasonableness" hardly solves the problem, however. The question now centers upon "notice of adverse claims." Hank Rohlf asked, "What constitutes notice? Is it official notice when a list is mailed out? Is it official when it reaches the mailroom of a company? Whose responsibility is it to see that the notice reaches those individuals who have to make a determination about a piece? How do you make sure that every branch office of every bank and brokerage house receives notice?"

Rohlf raised legitimate questions about the efficacy of any attempt to disseminate notice. And this weakness is the one that permits careless, greedy, or crooked bankers to lay claim to be holders in due course. They can argue that they failed to receive information indicating a piece was on a hot list.

Morgan Guaranty, its insurers, and its lawyers had wrestled with several alleged innocent holders in due course for more than five years by the close of 1975. And although the initial losses to the bank and its underwriters amounted to $723,000, Rohlf estimated that the final figure would be closer to $500,000.

Meanwhile, the criminal trials wound down. Three men, the West German Charles Lembertz, the Swiss Louis Amhof, and the U.S. citizen Joseph Lamattina (associate of

Vincent Teresa and Marvin Karger), remained fugitives
under indictment. More than sixty individuals had been
seized around the world in connection with the theft;
fewer than half actually went to trial. Still outstanding, and
presumably worthless, was a $1,000,000 piece, five
$100,000 notes, a $10,000, and a $1,000 note. From the
original packet of seventy-eight pieces, seventy had been
recovered.

With the possible exception of Marvin Karger, no individual was captured—nor were any T bills recovered—by
means of painstaking logical deductions based on clues, by
means of the endless strings of interviews, or through the
findings of a white-smocked crime lab technician. Instead,
the recovery of paper and the apprehension of an assorted
bag of yeggery depended upon either sharp-eyed officials
in financial institutions or the bane of all criminals, informers.

The performances of the houses of finance are not im-
pressive. Laidlaw & Company halted Lester Spivak's
move. The Chase Manhattan in New York picked up the
notes offered by Grant Scruggs and Henry Schumer. The
Mexico City branch of First National City of New York
tripped up Markowitz and Mulligan. Institutions in Luxembourg, Switzerland, and Sweden sundered the best-laid
plans of several miscreants.

However, the National Bank of North America in New
York apparently made only a superficial stab toward discovery of any notice of infirmity in the T bill shown in its
offices. Similarly, the National City Bank of Detroit failed
to recognize incipient chicanery in the machinations of
Melvin Markowitz. The Bahamian bank put through a
$500,000 piece without any qualms about the ownership.
Possibly these citadels of fiscal responsibility were the victims of misinformation. They could have been fed erroneous serial numbers or a clerk might have unwittingly transposed some figures. But the best evidence of testimony in

a number of trials was that the institutions did not check carefully and did not bother to retain current lists of pilfered securities. Similarly the conduct of the Town Bank and Trust in Brookline, Massachusetts, and the Irvington Branch of the First National State of New Jersey is questionable.

Ray Arthur's loan coup in New Jersey may indeed have been the tip of a big green iceberg. There is considerable likelihood that the Morgan loot served as collateral for loans issued by banks and brokerage firms. It is significant that the swindler's market was not suddenly glutted with Morgan Guaranty's missing T bills. Instead, they showed up for redemption in a steady stream. The organized crime fraternity is well aware that after maturity T bills lose their flavor of authenticity. It is unlikely that the stuff sat in a concealed drop or a safe deposit box where it could earn nothing. The logical conclusion is that after the bills, in some instances, had served their purpose for a short-term loan, they were dumped on suckers who tried to cash them.

The gallery of hustlers that appeared before the Senate Subcommittee looking into fraud and theft in securities cited innumerable instances in which filched paper provided the collateral for borrowed money. Careless executives, or friendly employees in a bank, risk very little by accepting a stolen security as a guarantee against a loan. The borrowers of organized crime are contented with the use of a bank's money for three months. There's no need to be greedy and risk capture as a result of absconding without paying off the debt. Since bank auditors seldom if ever examine the collateral to determine whether the owner who pledged it actually possessed a legal title, the opportunity to discover a cozy arrangement between banker and crook is nil.

The Morgan Guaranty caper triggered intensive analysis of the securities security problem. Wall Street and its allies in the banking world have realized that organized crime no longer regards the paper instruments of modern capitalism as a coarse substitute for toilet tissue. If there were any such doubts in the minds of bankers and brokers, the testimony before the Senate Subcommittee should have disabused them. Senator Edward Gurney, a member of the investigatory body, reported that "upwards of $400,000,000 in stolen securities [privately issued as well as government] had yet to be recovered for the years of 1969 and 1970. However, I can say—notwithstanding the efforts of the financial community—that the problem has gotten much worse. Statistics obtained from the Federal Bureau of Investigation show approximately $156,000,000 in U.S. government securities were reported stolen in the year 1973—which represents a 120 percent increase over 1972 figures, and the largest amount ever reported stolen since the inception of the FBI's stolen securities file. Likewise, data . . . by both stock exchanges, several banks and other financial entities, show that $104,000,000 worth of securities were reported as lost or stolen in 1973. This new figure represents a 434 percent increase over 1972, and again, the largest sum ever reported since 1967."

Senator Gurney also inserted into the record a statement from Lt. Robert Kappes, the commanding officer of the Bond and Forgery Squad in New York. Kappes listed $22,000,000 in lost or stolen securities reported to his unit for 1973. Of that amount only $3,000,000, or less than 15 percent, had been recovered.

The National Crime Information Center, a computerized data bank designed to assist law enforcement agencies, showed a steady increase in thefts of government obligations. In 1969 the amount was $77,000,000. It soared to $154,000,000 in 1971. The following year witnessed a sharp drop but in 1973 the thieves recouped with a haul of $148,000,000.

The highest guess on the amount of stolen securities

came from Securities Validation Corporation. A privately
funded profit-oriented creation of Sci Tek Inc., SVC attempted to sell as a service to banks, brokerage houses, insurance firms, and other interested parties an up-to-date,
computerized listing of all paper reported as lost or stolen.
Henry du Pont, chairman of the Securities Validation Corporation board, told the Senate Subcommittee that in 1974
his company's computer listed 800,000 securities, worth
approximately $11,000,000,000, as gone from their rightful
place. Based upon the number of clients SVC had, compared to the total number of firms dealing with securities,
du Pont said SVC was aware of 15 to 20 percent of what
actually was missing. The total of lost, strayed, or stolen
securities therefore approached $50,000,000,000, he said.

SVC, which hoped for federal legislation that would encourage companies to buy its services, was not a disinter-
ested observer. Witnesses from the financial community
disputed the figures, arguing that the totals were swollen
by inclusion of items that were only lost or misplaced.
These instruments often were quickly located.

Conceivably, du Pont's estimate could have been double the actual amount of unaccounted for paper. The
haggling over whether there is $25,000,000,000 or
$50,000,000,000 missing explains some of the nature of the
problem. The figures are so large that there is an absence
of reality. Like the federal budget, the concept of even
$25,000,000,000 orbits out of sight of human experience.
Not even David Rockefeller understands what it is to handle billions in real money, let alone cart it to a store and attempt to spend it.

When these enormous sums are removed one step from
currency and transformed into certificates, there is a second loss of meaning. Marvin Karger felt no thrill in fon-
dling a T bill nor did he experience a flush of prosperity.
But when he staggered out of the bank with $70,000 in $5

bills, Marvin Karger was intoxicated with a feeling of wealth.

If the wealthiest money managers in the nation cannot experience these hundreds of thousands of shares and notes as money, certainly the $125-a-week clerk of 1969 (or his $200-a-week counterpart today) would be hard-pressed to think of the paper on his desk as anything more than a commodity, like an order for two million links of sausage or a ton of steel. Also, the volume of big numbered certificates passing through the back rooms inevitably breeds contempt for the familiar. The fact is, a $20 bill would not be permitted to circulate in the offices of the money temples with the easy insouciance accorded a $100,000 T bill. It's not simply because one item appears more easily negotiable. The larger item loses its reality as a money instrument by virtue of its size and its one-step removal from the status of currency.

Several swindlers conned accomplices with the statement that the T bills were as good as cash. But they were *not* the same as cash and that was one of the factors that befuddled ordinarily sober-sided individuals. Were one to approach a businessman and offer him $25 if he could help change a $100 bill in a bank, he would summon either the law or a psychiatrist. However, when tempted with a $100,000 T bill for what amounted to a similar commission, respectable investors saw nothing amiss. Credit some of the confusion to the nature of paper instruments, as well as to avarice.

Securities Validation Corporation suggested that the most effective means to halt thefts would be a requirement that every transfer of paper must be checked through a central clearing house. A computer would check out serial numbers and other pertinent data to verify the ownership. Obviously that would limit knavery; it would also have guaranteed a profitable future for SVC.

Carl Klemme, executive vice president of Morgan
Guaranty (he replaced Rohlf on the latter's retirement)
strongly resisted the proposals of SVC. Voicing the sen-
timents of most of his contemporaries in the industry,
Klemme had no objection to a central listing of securities
that were known to be stolen or about which there was
some suspicion. However, when it came to a mandatory
check on all incoming securities, he quoted the former
president of the New York Stock Exchange's Stock Clearing Corporation: "In our depository . . . we receive some
20,000 securities every day which represents close to
100,000 individual certificates. It will take quite a computer operation to check 100,000 certificates just from that
one source."

Klemme said that at Morgan itself 10,000 certificates
passed through the custody section daily. Quite often the
turn-around time for securities transactions is limited to a
few hours. The paper work necessary to question the computer properly would destroy the ability of the banks and
brokerage houses to act swiftly enough to keep the paper-
fueled economy stoked. Just keeping the data bank up to
date would be an enormous job. Although none of the men
who spoke for the greatest names in U.S. finance ever
mentioned it, the slowdown would also have seriously cut
into the profits of the industry.

There is a parallel to the position taken. Department
stores suffering large losses to shoplifters could reduce
thefts greatly through several measures. According to an
executive in charge of protecting such establishments, limited access and egress in a department store would solve
much of the problem. A system of close inspection of all
packages taken from the stores along with more guards,
particularly in rest rooms and fitting rooms, would halt
much of the stealing. But the costs of such a program plus
the customer ill-will outweighs the benefits in the minds

of the proprietors. The situation is the same for the financial business.

There are those who take a less than charitable view of the opinions expressed by the representatives of banks and brokerage firms before the Subcommittee. An insurance company executive (his organization must underwrite losses by security transfer agents and the custodians of paper wealth) said, "I take violent exception to what was said. They simply want to avoid any kind of real data bank operation that could make them potentially liable. As it is, so long as an institution has given value and not operated illegally, then it's not liable for the sale of a stolen security. I think the insurance companies have buried their heads in the sand by failing to pressure for greater security, including data banks.

"I am convinced that the argument about slowing down the volume is a smoke screen. What might really hit the banks hard would be mandatory checking of what is offered as collateral for loans. That's where the criminals are making their best use of stolen securities and that's where the companies find their greatest earnings."

One of the points scored against the SVC plan was that alternative ways to check out dubious paper do exist. In New York, for example, if one of the twelve clearing house banks becomes suspicious of some certificates, it can query Lieutenant Kappes. As head of the Bond and Forgery Squad, he would obligingly inquire of the National Crime Information Center about the questionable pieces. Since the NCIC is plugged into law enforcement agencies only, the banks can not go directly to it.

The weakness of the arrangement is the limitation to the dozen highest ranking institutions. Thousands of branch offices of banks and brokerage houses are in no position to wait for one of the clearing house banks to forward their requests to Lieutenant Kappes.

In California, the Bank of America with 1,000 satellite offices agreed that mandatory checking of securities would be an intolerable burden. To protect itself against loans issued against possibly stolen securities, however, Bank of America's policy requires that borrowers have other qualifications beyond collateral in order for a loan to be approved. In addition, loans are not to be made unless the "identity and responsibility" of the borrower can be well established. Strictures of this nature have their limitations, obviously. Town Bank and Trust in Brookline made its loans to Lee and Allen whose identities and responsibilities were known to the bank. Nevertheless, better than $1.7 million was paid out against stolen T bills.

One major step toward the elimination of securities thefts has been the development with the Federal Reserve banks of a computerized book entry system for Treasury obligations. In this arrangement there is no actual paper transfer. Instead, sales and purchases are recorded in the computers. Since no notes exist, there is, theoretically, nothing for an employee to steal, or for the felons to negotiate. Perhaps 75 percent of the Treasury obligations that now move among the largest participants in the market exist only in terms of electronic messages.

Another measure that hopefully reduces the potential for security thefts has been the creation of the Depository Trust Company of New York (similar operations have been started in Chicago and California). Here the aim is not the elimination of the documents, as in a book entry program, but immobilization of the pieces. Theoretically, that curtails the opportunities for thieves to lay hands on the items as they are traded. The DTC acts as a central agency for custody of $75,000,000,000 in stock certificates. The sales, purchases, and related money matters are all processed entries in DTC's books. As a result, DTC estimates it dispenses with three-quarters of the physical handling that offers opportunities to would-be traffickers in hot paper.

DTC is subject to the same sort of inside job threat that did in Morgan Guaranty. However, to forestall such losses, the operation exercises strict daily inventory audits. Microfilms of every certificate, front and back, help provide a reference in the event of any discrepancy. Furthermore, DTC holds much of its stock in "jumbo" certificates. These are in extremely large denominations and they serve much as street name stocks do for the brokerage houses. DTC's jumbos are considerably larger than the street name pieces and those worth $2,000,000 or more require a very special kind of endorsement making it nearly impossible for anyone to employ them illegally. Jumbos are also impregnated with a special substance that is supposed to trigger an alarm whenever a jumbo arrives at a transfer point in the depository, a spot where the piece is most vulnerable to disappearance.

The certificateless society by means of a total book entry system is a prospect of unlikely futurism. Many investors still desire the capacity to have physical contact with a tangible instrument of their wealth. Indeed, book entry is not even necessarily thief-proof. Book entry arrangements only demand a change in the criminal tactics. Instead of suborning a counting room clerk, the larcenous will have to buy the loyalty of a computer mechanic or a programmer. Given the ways of computer technology, it's conceivable that bigger and harder-to-unravel capers may follow if a skilled technician manipulates the computer for his benefit. If book entry methods spread, the criminal wave of the future will be in escapades such as the multimillion dollar theft of city checks in Los Angeles, informed on by Mike Raymond, in which the computer issued checks cashable by the swindlers.

Similarly, it's unlikely that total immobilization of America's paper instruments can be achieved. Various rules of the Securities and Exchange Commission, the exigencies of capital expansion, the needs and desires of customers and brokers all conspire to restrict what will be stored in a DTC arrangement.

The reforms of book entry for Treasury obligations and the role of the Depository Trust Company plus the stubborn resistance to any mandatory checking apparatus doomed the Securities Validation Corporation, even as its board chairman bravely addressed the Senate Subcommittee. SVC's failure to sign up even one-fifth of the traders in securities meant that its usefulness was dubious. For all of the successes reported by the self-proclaimed savior of the financial community, it could not adequately finance itself, and SVC ceased operations in January, 1975. Some SVC defenders accused the banks and brokerage houses of operating a club that blackballed any business critical of them. Hank Rohlf scoffed that it was simply a case of a company that could not demonstrate enough earning power to justify loans to it.

The platoon of financial executive v.p.'s that trooped to Washington to inform the Senate Subcommittee had other recommendations, apart from innovations like book entry and DTC. Painfully cognizant that on numerous occasions employees had been keys to thefts, the witnesses asked for more freedom to investigate the workers. Specifically, they asked repeatedly for the right to have fingerprints and backgrounds of job applicants checked against the files of law enforcement agencies, including the FBI. Currently, private organizations, with few exceptions, do not have legal access to the records kept by the lawmen. In fact, some cops have accepted payoffs in return for supplying background information on candidates for positions in a company.

The value of fingerprint checks and the use of name checks against criminal records in order to screen prospective employees is highly questionable. The investigations after the Morgan Guaranty robbery, which matched fingerprints of suspects and probed into the backgrounds of the custody section workers, failed to identify The Person. There is no evidence that The Person ever had a criminal dossier. For that matter, several of the outsiders arrested and convicted for their roles in the crime had no previous encounters with the police. Any thoughtful thief who occupies a sensitive position in a financial house realizes that if he has a record he automatically becomes the prime suspect.

Finally, why should banks and brokerage firms have any more right to pry into the lives of employees than that accorded other industries subject to theft? In a nation allegedly devoted to civil liberties and individual freedom, the attempt to erode these primary values for the sake of money and its instruments is an ugly sacrifice to Mammon. Protection of the goods left to the safekeeping of the financial community ought to remain dependent upon strictly enforced controls rather than invasions of the private lives of human beings.

The proponents for sanitizing the work force also asked for the power to require polygraphs of employees. Hundreds of Morgan Guaranty employees waived their right of refusal to be hooked to a lie detector machine after the T bills disappeared. Jerry Lascala in fact took two polygraphs in an effort to prove his innocence. The machines discovered no evidence. Mandatory polygraphs would clearly appear to be a violation of the Fifth Amendment's protection against self-incrimination.

The visitors to Washington also asked that all security thefts become subject to federal law. In most instances that is a formality. Any hanky-panky with a Treasury obligation is by definition a federal crime; any theft from a bank covered by the Federal Depositors Insurance is a federal crime and it would seem that any stolen security under regulation by the Securities and Exchange Commission would become a federal offense.

Heavier punishment for perpetrators of securities thefts was another near unanimous request. It might decirculate some of the perennials in the hot paper trade but there does not seem to be any shortage of willing thieves and fixers prepared to fill any employment gaps. The bankers and brokers cried shame at the plea bargaining that goes on. But often that is a function of the system of informers who are the key to the recovery of securities. The mechanism of the informer is a perplexing one. Joe Leahy, drawing on his experience with the New York Bond and Forgery Squad said, "The payments to informers stimulate people to steal. I know of a case where the word was that the company would pay five points for anything returned to it. People went out and took the stuff just for the five points." Hank Rohlf insisted his organization would not pay for information and recovery unless it were accompanied by an arrest. Other firms and law enforcement agencies are not that finicky. One result is the helpful fellows who continue to practice what they peach on.

The balance sheet for the industry proposals to the Subcommittee adds up to a serious effort to control thefts by book entry and immobilization of securities along with some frivolous, if not dangerous recommendations that would shift the ultimate responsibility for safekeeping onto the law enforcement agencies. There is no sign of any willingness to accept methods that limit the freedom of bankers or brokers. At the very least, traders in securities ought to know the background of a borrower, at least as much as they desire to know the backgrounds of their employees.

The answer to the question of how to prevent replays of the Morgan Guaranty caper calls for an appraisal of the cast of characters in that crime. The prerequisite for negotiation of large amounts of stolen securities is organized crime. To remove the paper from safekeeping is no great trick; the payoff lies in conversion into cash. One cannot casually approach a bank or brokerage firm to dispose of a hot piece worth $100,000. The task requires an intimate knowledge of the securities market, the personnel, the way things can be done without leaving a trail for cops and feds. Organized crime—with its fences, its liaisons in the legitimate world, and its international connections—has the necessary web to move hot paper.

Starting with Marvin Karger, the participation of organized crime in the negotiations of the T bills was clearly visible. Many other episodes have obvious threads to the mob: Benny Marchese in the Luxembourg caper had ties, as did Samuel Schwartz's supplier in the double agent deal, Louis Pergola. Robert Hite mentioned "the old man in Buffalo," when he spoke to porn merchant Bernard Reindolph. Vincent Poerio, Anthony Tavolaris, John Lusterino, and Lazzaro San Giovanni all had the right associations. Marvin Mulligan's long-distance call from Mexico City went to a Brooklyn hangout of Mafia members. In cases where the tracings were less readily apparent, circumstances pointed toward organized crime. Manny Lester never personally stuffed a wad of securities in his brief case and walked out of a back room of some brokerage house. Someone else did the stealing; Manny Lester went to Toronto then to peddle the paper. Only organized crime has the ability to seek out a Lester and vice versa.

The score of the feds against organized crime in the Morgan Guaranty caper is frustrating. Jack Mace, part of the ring feeding T bills to Karger in Boston, and probably the best catch, was not a member. But as a top fence he provided greater service to the mob than any of the low-level types who were caught. At best Benny Marchese and Vincent Poerio, who serviced Stuart Norman and Anthony Tavolaris, were insignificant soldiers. Ranking members of the Cosa Nostra families were untouched. "They place so many levels between themselves and the stolen stuff," complained a prosecutor, "that you never get close to making a case against them."

Then there were the fringe people, the small-time hustlers. Marvin Karger was a typical victim. He ran the major risk, appearing at the bank and actually collecting the money. He earned for himself the toughest sentence handed out, twelve years. The federal prisons are well populated with Marvin Kargers, the natural handmaidens of organized crime. They share with their betters a common attitude that provides a real bond. The brotherhood of organized crime and its auxiliaries are the quintessential specimens of a cash nexus society. What counts is the score, not how you played the game. The rules or laws are an effort by others to limit the competition. Karger's only regret when it all ended was that his connections had cheated him of a portion of the take. Likewise, Vincent Teresa began to talk only after Joe Lamattina fled with the contents of a safe deposit box he shared with Teresa.

Another set of actors in the drama was personified by Stuart Norman, the vending machine entrepreneur who took a disastrous flyer with Tavolaris and Poerio. He was the desperate businessman who took his first false step. It was notable, incidentally, that the T bills were all on his person when he was arrested. Folks with experience do their best to keep their hands off the goods in case of a bust. Melvin Markowitz, as part of the M and M boys south of the border, strongly resembles Stuart Norman. He too was a businessman teetering on the edge of failure. The only difference is that he refused to cooperate with the government and as a result bought himself a full five-year term, unlike Norman. White middle-class Americans, Norman and Markowitz, oriented to a certain kind of financial success, could not resist the opportunity to save themselves with a fast dishonest dollar. They were like victims of a viral infection, individuals whose normal immunity had been sapped by fiscal decline. Based upon the Morgan Guaranty experience, as well as that of other swindles, immunization of respectables is not something to be taken for granted, particularly in times of economic stress.

Six years after the theft, only the barest residue of the World Series caper remains. By 1976 only Anthony Tavolaris, Vincent Poerio, Salvatore Cuomo, and Benny Marchese will still be behind bars. Joel West, having done his time for bank robbery and possession of stolen securities, is now a free man. Grant Scruggs, who accused West, at last report was in the insurance business, while Henry Schumer, the other witness against West, worked in Florida. Jack Mace and Arthur Tortorello, who was busted on charges that came from evidence on the wire taps, both get their freedom in 1976. Marvin Mulligan and Melvin Markowitz similarly can count on release around that time. Bernard Reindolph is back in Canada still selling porn, and his Swedish associates are also out of jail.

The FBI men who worked on the case have long since gone on to other matters. A number of the young, aggressive Strike Force prosecutors have left government service to practice privately. Tom Dolan, Joe Leahy, and Benjamin Rhoades all retired from the New York City police and became security supervisors for companies in the stock and bond trade. Tom Dolan, in fact, replaced the late Eugene Golden, who had been in command at Morgan Guaranty at the time of the robbery.

Ronald Duffy continues to put in long hours to keep the paper moving, safely, at Morgan Guaranty. He has not

forgotten what happened. "I lie awake nights trying to figure out the security system, how someone can beat it.
Then I plan ways to prevent someone from beating it. I
take losses personally, it's my pride."

Hank Rohlf enjoys his retirement, spending a day each
week at the bank when he's not in Florida playing golf,
fishing, or riding a bicycle. But he hasn't forgotten either.
"I still think about what happened. I'd like to see the guy
who did it locked up. More than that, I guess I'd really
like to know how he actually did it. Goddamit, they can
always get you if they want to."

And The Person? Jerry Lascala had been the chief suspect but after three months of suspension he returned to
work at the bank in another capacity. Among those who interceded for him was Hank Rohlf. Until The Person is un-
masked, a shadow hangs over Lascala. But Hank Rohlf
believes in Lascala and feels someone else is guilty.

The Person may still toil in the back rooms of Morgan
Guaranty. It is also possible that once the fuss died away,
The Person quietly left the company to enjoy the spoils.
One thing is certain, no one is searching for The Person
any longer. For whatever profit or purpose, The Person
has gotten away with the World Series caper.